TABLE OF CONTENTS

INTRODUCTION

E motions and moods, represents a significant role in the journey of being a great in leadership. However, many are confused about the nature of emotions and how important it is to recognize the different kinds of emotions.

Firstly, what is emotion?

According to Marriam Webster dictionary, emotions is a conscious mental reaction that is subjectively experienced as a strong feeling which is usually directed to a specific object and typically accompanied by physiological and behavioral changes in the body. What this means is that emotions are inevitable and unavoidable. It is the very essence of what makes a living being and distinguishes from the dead because with 'experience', e.g. death of loved one, the **reactive feeling** to that **cause** is identified by emotion.

The Diagram below shows the different kinds of emotions with the circular surface of the prism representing the most basic form of emotions.

Figure 1- Plutchik's Wheel of Emotions

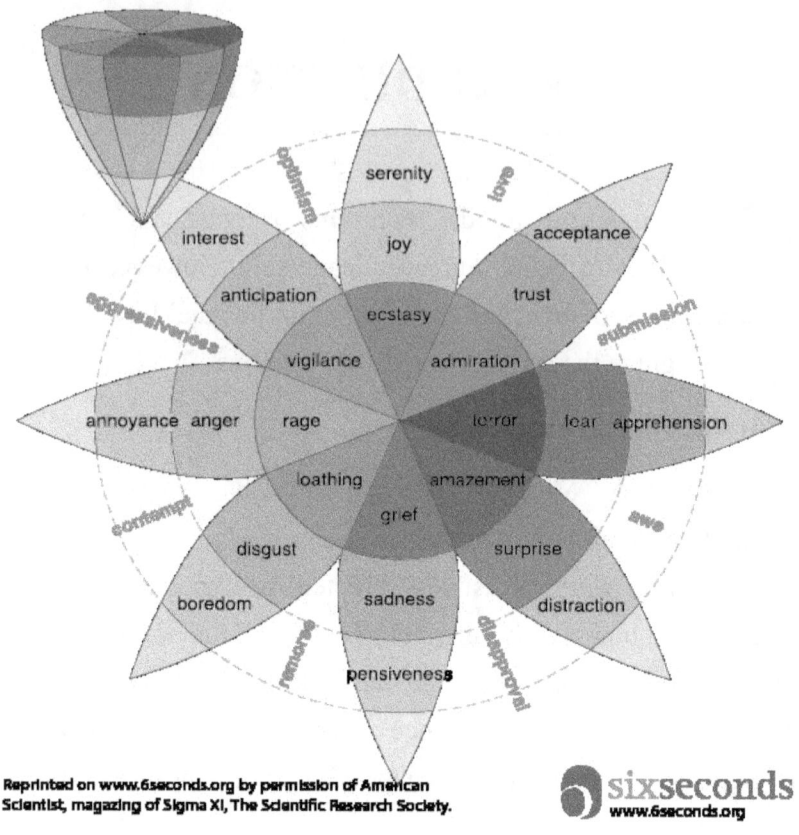

Identifying Emotions

1. Ecstasy: This is a feeling of intense joy and Happiness. This word originated from Greek, meaning 'total involvement of either a subject or object of interest. It could be easily believed as a default feeling (i.e how one should feel all the time) since it is perceived as harmless. However, this point is discredited considering that complete involvement in one thing isn't normal because one must also be aware of other objects/subject with unbiased judgement. This feeling is what fuels culture, religion and even politics. It is triggered by the *focus* of an object.

2. Admiration: This is popularly characterized by unconscious formulation/acquisition of social relationships and values. It encourages self-improvement and motivation. It is triggered by *the Ideal* of an object. There are many ways this kind of emotion can be identified. The most common are:

i.   Imitation of role models

ii.   Sexual attraction

iii.   Compassion to others

3. Terror: This a particular feeling that cuts across most living organism (I.e. Aside humans, other animals experience and exhibit this emotion). It is triggered by *threat and danger* of an object. Behavioral reaction to fear or apprehension can differ from person to person due to the level of threat/danger perceived by the respective persons. For example- one person may fight a snake while the other may flee. Fear and anxiety/apprehension are usually characterized as weak feelings because it is a defensiveness.

4. Amazement: This feeling is a product of *unusual and unexpected* events. This psychological state is brief and may be either a pleasant or unpleasant. The flexibility of this emotion can be seen at instances that involves other types of emotion (i.e. one may feel surprised before feeling these emotions and not limited to terror or admiration).

5. Grief: Scientist and Psychologist research that there 5 main stages of grief with each having a separate emotion. However, the predominant emotion is sadness/depression. Grief is caused by the *loss* of an object. There are numerous methods of dealing with grief and it varies in different people and affected by factors like a person's personality, life experiences or even the significance of the object/subject loss. Time in feeling Grieve also vary.

6. Loathing: when someone feels intense hatred/dislike/disgust for something or someone, this emotion is described as loathing. This feeling is completely anonymous to love and admiration. However, when one feels esthetic, it may be accompanied by loathing if not, admiration. Emotional literacy is described as Identifying one's feelings at a particular moment when triggered by a cause. It does not only mean labeling by words but most importantly, being aware of how the various forms of emotions intersect and interact with one another.

7. Rage: this emotion is recognized physically by an increase in blood pressure and heart rate while experiencing disgust/contempt of an object. Its default response is hostility. A large number of reports distinguishes anger as the most harmful state of mind as it has many mental and physical consequences compared to other forms of emotions.

8. Vigilance: This emotion is triggered by a *prolonged curiosity* of an object. It could result advantageous or disadvantageous depending on how it is applied. For example, Paranoia is a harmful state resulting from this emotion. But thus, anticipation creates a level of productivity individually and in organization. Nevertheless, vigilance, however being applied, always demands a sense of security.

Emotional literacy is described as Identifying one's feelings at a particular moment when triggered by a cause. It does not only mean labeling by words but most importantly, being aware of how the various forms of emotions intersect and interact with one another.

Clinical Study of Emotions

Emotions are woven together with life experience. These different feelings stated above are the basics to survive in the ecosystem. In humans, it is effective whereby these natural feelings provide important information so as to enable appropriate action in any situation. Tor Wager, the director of cognitive neuroscience laboratory at The University of Colorado, says that emotions are vital to psychopathology and other various diseases.

Although while science researchers are discovering why emotions are applicable in all parts of behavioral, cognition and health, there still remain challenges of integrating the brain to process this information. Anyone who had felt either of these emotions like anger or happiness can tell of how overwhelmed with feelings. This is because emotions excite the nervous system resulting to changes in respiration, heart rate and facial/body expression.

However, in as much as emotions are easily recognizable when seen or felt, when scientists conduct an experiment using FMRI (functional magnetic resonance imaging) to identify and tag these various feelings, it is difficult. Wagner points out the difficulty is in the limitation of emotional stimuli provided in an enclosed lab. For example, while FMRI captures a disgust facial expression triggered by a photograph, the degree of angry emotions may differ with real life experiences (i.e. compared to when a stranger annoys one in a public train).

Just as another experiment was carried out by a neuroscientist, Marcel Just, and his colleagues at Carnegie Mellon University, where some students at the drama department were asked to experience and express various emotions. It was discovered that these students reacted with different emotions.

This discovery now imposes a new question. Does it mean that emotions are subjective from person to person? i.e. regarding personalized experiences, does the feeling happiness or contempt processed differently? Can these mental states- emotions, be trained and control with conscious processes?

Emotional Intelligence-How is Emotion Triggered?

A career in aerospace is probably the rarest and most difficult job to achieve in which space organization such as NASA employs only a few dozen in decades. One has to be the very best in every area of life including and not limited to physical, intellect and social responsibilities.

Nina Fowler was an astronaut that fit these requirements very excellently. She received a master's degree in aerospace engineering and furthered with postgraduate in astrophysics. She flew planes for U.S Navy for over 8 years and in a few years after embarking on missions, she became a selected few to become an astronaut.

Obviously, she was an intelligent woman. However, when she found out about her lover's affair with another woman, Nina drove her Mercedes 16 hours to Huston in attempt to confront her rival. Nina packed duck tapes, pepper spray and a garbage bags- a vague but unthoughtful plan to abduct the other woman. But when approaching the other woman's car, Nina experience an emotional breakdown, exposing her to authority that warranted her arrest.

In the 1980s, researchers came up with a concept called *Emotional Intelligence* to explain the reasons intelligent people like

Nina will often act stupidly. It based its credibility on the notion that general intelligence (IQ) is a measure of one's capacity to process and understand information while emotional intelligence (EQ) is one's capacity to process and understand emotions. This ability-emotional intelligence- mustn't be limited to one's own emotions but also in knowing and understanding other people's emotions.

A book written by Daniel Goleman on this subject highlight why and how EQ is a vital sauce in leadership. The psychologist states that the chances of achieving success is greatly influenced by the ability to understand and manage feelings/emotions.

But how can emotional intelligence be recognized and adapted in daily life?

The image below illustrates how information is being processed in the man brain.

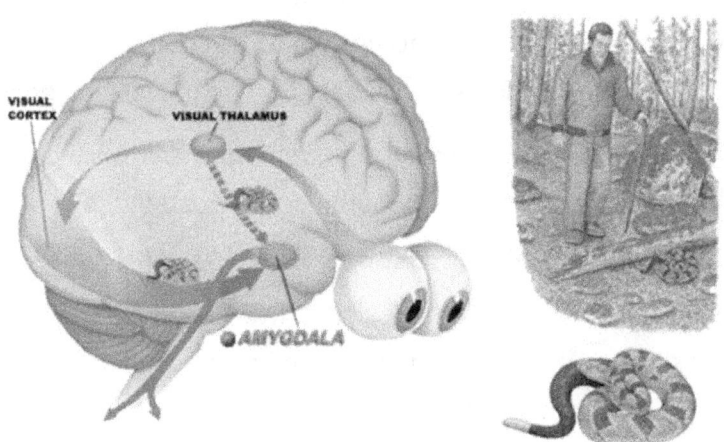

Illustration based on LeDoux JE (1994) Emotion, Memory, and the Brain. Scientific American.

Figure 2- Limbic System illustrating emotional response

The amygdala is an almond-shaped nucleus that is located in the temporal lobe and that is responsible for the fight or flight responses when encountering an object. It serves like the brain circuit box where decisions on how to react to a certain object are stored. When in contact with a threat, the thalamus which is responsible for receiving data (in the form of stimuli), transmit these stimuli to the cortex. The cortex takes its time to process these data thoroughly before transporting the information to the amygdala.

However, as its been scientifically proven, signals cannot be 100% transported from one point to another. This simply means that while the thalamus sends out data to the cortex, a quantity of this data is also being received by the amygdala. Noting that the amygdala is designed for action and not reasoning. This explains how impulse/instincts are felt.

For example, a man sees a snake and his first instinct is to fight. However, if he could take a few seconds to reason, he may find out that the snake is a large distance away and he could easily avoid the stress by fleeing- which is a reasonable action in that situation.

This is what distinguishes leaders from the mass. It's their ability to reason and apply emotional intelligence. Moreover, this is not an easy task to do. It requires discipline and control of mind/emotion.

In this book, we will discuss what it means to be emotionally free and how leaders are able to manage and discipline their emotions.

CHAPTER ONE
DISCIPLINED LEADERSHIP

What is Leadership?

" A leader is one who knows the way, goes the way, and shows the way" John C Maxwell

Great leaders are those with vision and an ability to pull people towards that vision. They make that difference between failure and success. There have been popular debates about whether leaders are born or made. However, one thing is certain- Anybody can be a leader but leadership isn't for everybody. This simply means that one who isn't a leader but aspires to become one can learn to do so.

Characteristics of a Good Leader

1.   **Excellent Communicator**- The book by Dale Carnegie, `How to win friends and influence people', stresses on the importance of this point. It explains how great leaders attains the ability to not only speak effectively in private and in public, but most importantly, how to listen and understand other people speak.

2.   **Confidence**- He or She must first believe in themselves before compelling others to believe. Leaders are known to have a strong sense of power by simply being comfortable in their skin.

3.   **Time Management**- Time is valuable, and leaders are known to place this value very high, even higher than money. Managing 24hrs a day isn't as simple but by creating a list of high

priority task, sharing these tasks to appropriate time per day or per week, one will achieve greater success rate rather than not managing time at all.

4.   **Innovation**- Leaders are easily spotted by their creativity and unique in how they think. They are the revolutionist. This must only be exercised in grandeur but in simple daily tasks. Problems arise every day whether domestically or professionally and it is a leader's duty to find a solution in every possible way.

5.   **Delegation and empowerment**- This characteristic works together with time management. Leaders aware of their capacity and their limitations to execute task. This is why they need to maintain a good relationship with people. A popular quote says that a great king is one who knows his court. This means that a leader must not only take account of his abilities but also the ability of others. This will come in handy in a situation where tasks are reassigned to people- *to the right people.*

6.   **Positivity and Energetic**- Everybody wants to be around people with positive energy. Emotions/Moods can be infectious. Robert Greene ascribed this law to Number ten in the 48 laws of power. It explains how people avoid the unhappy and unlucky as a natural phenomenon. Likewise, people are most attracted to happiness and luck. In leadership, there must be followers, this is unavoidable.

7.   **Passion and commitment**- It is one thing to begin a course, and it is a totally different thing to see it to the very end. Leaders strive in this aspect of finishing what was started. They carry out their tasks with great zeal and focus.

8.   **Honesty and Integrity**- One vital trait about great leaders is trustworthiness. When a leader successfully gains their follower's

trust, the rest is history- they are able to move towards their vision without resistance. Leaders are great examples of what is known as "practicing what one preaches".

9.   **Accountability**- being accountable means being responsible for decisions made. NO EXCUSE. Leaders know that every decision must be made wisely because at the end of the day, they must answer to a troublesome question- "What did you achieve today?"

10.   **Empathy**- leaders must live by example. They must show compassion in both mind and body. Amongst all the points, this play a most important condition in being a great leader. This is where emotional intelligence come into play. Knowing and understanding one's emotions while learning, understanding, and controlling the emotions of others- hence managing the emotional affair of a course.

Leadership involves mastering oneself and the affairs of followers. When becoming a leader, it is as important to also take into consideration the different types of dealing with situations. This flexibility is applicable where a successful tactic in one experience may turn unsuccessful in another experience. For example; An employee's manner in dealing with his employer must be completely different in dealing with his colleagues.

7 Disciplines of Leadership

1.   **Autocratic Leadership**- This is what is practiced by the authoritarian. Generally, all the responsibility in asserting power and authority is given to one person. There is little or no input by the team/subordinates of which the roles/tasks of each member is dictated by one head. The main difference of this type of leadership

from dictatorship is that autocracy, permits only one person with complete power while dictatorship can be one person or a group of people. Example, kings and queens employs this tactic in leading their kingdoms.

This is a rigid leadership practice therefore, being clear and assertive is important for decision-making. Although it I could be beneficial in the affairs of a company or a nation, in most cases, subordinates feel powerless and demoralized. Successful authoritarians recognize and effectively address this clause.

2.   **Charismatic Leadership**- This the strives on a leader's ability to inspire and transform the thoughts and attitude of others- in case of organization, its followers. The vision of the leader is vaguely adopted by the infected and all work together in achieving a common goal- that which was inspired by one person. It is Passive-aggressive in nature. For example, a church leader is charismatic in dealing with the congregation. He/she knows that the followers are not obligated to remain under the supervision of the head and gaining followership relies majorly on belief and energy. Unlike authoritarian leadership that is forceful and aggressive by nature.

3.   **Transformational Leadership**-just like charismatic leadership holds its influence by inspiration and motivation, transformational leaders also adapt the same tactics of dealing but unlike the former, this type of leadership doesn't require physical presence to effect change. It's often the case when the both kind of leadership is used simultaneously. An example of transformational leadership can be found in stars and heroes. It's stories of them ignites change.

4.   **Laissez-faire Leadership**- It is most common in the professional sectors where there is a high level of autocracy coupled

with a degree of transactional leadership. Here, employees are entrusted to carry out tasks that are for the benefit of the organization without direct order form the authoritarian (the boss). This type of leadership is successful when a company/organization assigns the right people to a specific position. It's an indirect method of infusing autocracy. For example, bank marketers are given a target to generate X number of funds by the end of each month. However, they venture to achieving that goal is left for the marketer to decide but although, the target was originally placed by the boss and will only be altered by the boss.

5.   **Transactional Leadership**- in a transactional type, a follower's loyalty relies heavily on the value of transaction. In the case of profitable organization, an employee is obligated to obey the leader when he/she accepted the job. However, when the employee resigns or the employer relieves duty, the employee will in turn be released from all obligations. Here, roles are clear and defined. Rewards and punishments are dependent on the degree of how well the job is carried out.

Note that this type of leadership is tightly limited to professionalism but not necessarily limited to companies and organizations. It could be vaguely applied in domestic circumstances like babysitting or lawn-mowing and in other cases.

6.   **Supportive Leadership**- leaders using this method delegate tasks and also provide means to achieving the goal. It is a more compassionate method than the transactional type. For example, a parent/guardian pays student tuition with an expectation that the student pass that academic session with good grades. They will further into providing food and housing allowance because it may increase the chances of achieving the common goal. However,

"to what degree?" is vaguely understood between the two parties. Some parents will support with only tuition and some will support to the very point of buying course handouts. Here there is also a vague expectation. If there were concrete and clear expectations, it becomes transactional and therefore loses all meaning of compassion. Professionally, it is not advisable to rely solely on this leadership strategy. Another example of how leaders employ this tactic is seen in non-profitable organizations like relief aids and even churches.

7.   **Democratic Leadership**- in this strategy, everybody is both leaders and followers. The emphasis is on equality. Ideas are being shared and discussed with unbiased opinion approach when executing plans. Members of this type of leadership are entrusted to act in benefit of all others but not obligated to do so. It encourages and promotes creativity in family, companies and organizations. An example of democratic leadership is seen in the united states of America where the government acts on fair and equal rights of the citizens.

The above listed are in constant use of a complexity of emotions. One must have mastered the emotions of both themselves and of others to be able to successfully execute these power tactics.

It must also be noted that the level of passivity and aggression in employing these tactics are flexible as well. For example, for obvious reasons, Charismatic leadership is easily applicable in leading a church, there will be cases where church workers (staff member or volunteers) will respond effectively to a transactional form of leadership. The secret is knowing when and how to apply these types of leadership.

However, what happens when emotions get in the way of

successful executing these strategies? When charisma is needed to address the congregation, what then happens if the pastor isn't just having a good day?

CHAPTER TWO
DISTINGUISHING BETWEEN
FREEDOM AND DISCIPLINE

Swiss psychiatrist, Carl Jung, in one of his researches, described Individualism as development of one's consciousness. It is an identity- when a person carves out its uniqueness which is distinguished from society norm. The active word here is 'consciousness', 'self-realization' and 'personalization' whereby one becomes aware of their uniqueness. Jung notion applies to individuals as a member of group and not as an isolated existence.

Society plays an essential role in life experiences. In the experiment carried out by Jung, self-conscious individuals impressed a positive relationship with the group. Here, the self-conscious person allows himself to grasp the subconsciousness of the group and respond with intentional expression and manner.

Society provides institutions like family, schools and marriage, and not limited, so as to ensure the formation of individuality. The greatest threat for a person seeking individualism is conformity. Individualism will only manifest when one makes decision not because society demands the act but because he/she thinks the decision is right. The active word here is "choice". This requires a high level of confidence and responsibility which is unavoidable in both leadership and followership. Individualism is a most vital constitution of freedom.

Culture and Behavior of Individualism

People's thoughts and behavior are highly influenced by culture. A factor in studying cross culture involves similarities between collective culture and that which is individualistic. Differences in both cultural formations are also significant in these studies.

In individualism, the culture is majorly influenced by an individual's value over a group/society. Here, an individual exerts his/her independence and maintains autonomy of power- The boss is self. The person's behavior depends less on society expectations and more on individual preferences. Western Europe are popular for its individualistic culture.

For example, the Pop-culture of a typical African-American musician living in Detroit is Rap/RnB. However, there are cases where other Genre, like classical music, are adapted by musicians of similar racial type and geolocation. This difference, although exists, are very few and it is greatly influenced by society institution, e.g. community groups like schools and faith organizations.

The table below shows the difference between Individualistic Culture and Societal Culture:

	Individualism	Society
1	Person's right take center stage	Society standards take center stage
2	Highest value placed on person's independence	Highest value placed on socialization
3	Person is more self-reliant	Person is socially dependent
4	Person is unique	Person conforms to society norm

The likelihood to focus attention on a person's identity is a pervasive aspect of culture which has a serious influence on the effectiveness of societal function. For example, a person who subscribes to individualism will often value their own culture and well-being over that imposed by the group. Unlike a Group's culture (collective culture) in which people make sacrificing of displeasing themselves for the benefit of everyone. This differences between individualism and society affects human behaviors in all sectors including career choices, product affiliation and responsiveness to social issues.

Cross-culture psychologist are now becoming very aware of the great influence that cultural/behavior have on a person's mental state and vice versa. However, an issue arises when individual preference/choice/culture may cause harm to the greater number of collectives/societies.

"It isn't what you have or who you are or where you are or what you are doing that makes you happy or unhappy. It is what you think about it." _ Dale Carnegie

Social Expectations and Social Norms

A society can be described as a group of people/individuals that are in continuous interactions socially and culturally. This group share a larger ideology aside which may or may not differ from personal ideals. These ideals could be formed politically, geographically, culturally or religiously. It could be affected by and not limited to class, race and even gender. The very essence of society structure is "grouping" individualism.

Society can influence one's behavior in many ways. The most common and predominant is the expectation of one's group/society. Often times, we expect others to act in a particular way and in a particular situation.

Often times, we expect others to act in a particular way and in a particular situation. Every society has an expected and proper way for people to behave. These expectations vary from one social group to another. A person in a particular group is expected to adopt these standard behaviors whether they like it or not. People often find it emotionally overwhelming to deal with such situations whereby how they feel about something is different about how society feels about it.

"All the worlds a stage,

And all the men and women merely players:

They have their exits and their entrances;

And one man in these times play many parts." _ William Shakespeare

What this poem captures are the social roles imposed by a single man. Imagine all the types of role you have to play in daily in your life. For example, a father, a mother, a son, an employee, a student, a friend, etc. every role has an expected way a person must behave which is referred to as social norm.

10 Most Popular Social Norms

1. One should be very popular and have a lot of friends

2. One must have a social media account and should remain active all the time.

3. One must be very good, an expert in fact, at some type of skill.

4. One should be doing something highly productive all the time.

5. One shouldn't be single but must be in a serious relationship that leads to marriage

6. One should be happy all the time and remain smiling always

7. One should plan to do certain types of things at a certain age e.g. graduate from university before age 25, get married before 30 and have a retirement plan before 60.

8. One should according to how they look and dress

9. On should have a particular type of view that is according

to their family background and income.

10. One should be a graduate of a college or university

A high level of pressure exists where a person attains conformity to these unspoken/unwritten rules. Many of us are constantly dealing the right way to feel about these rules and whether we must accept conformity or not.

Society is a structure that has been in existence since the beginning of man. It has been, still is, and will be, the standard rule book, so it's impossible to act as though it doesn't exist. However, it must not be mandatory to follow these set of rules as long as it doesn't cause harm to others.

For example, in America, it is legal to own a gun but illegal to shoot a person just because one is having a bad day. However, the shooting can be justified in self-defense of the other being shot.

Understanding Human Rights and Freedom

Human rights are basic sets of freedom and choices owned by every person/human from the time of birth to the time of death. Its applicable irrespective of place of origin or religion. They are rights that cannot be taken away by any larger authority, only restricted, e.g. in criminal cases.

These set of rights have common values:

1. Dignity

2. Fairness

3. Respect

4. Independence

They are well defined and are protected by state law.

Identifying these values as rights of every member of the human race is the essence of peace and justice in the world.

a)   Everyone is born equal and free with their own dignity and their rights. They are bestowed with consciousness and reasoning; therefore, they should act in respect amongst themselves in spirited brotherhood.

b)   Everybody has rightful claims to the freedom stated here, and without any distinction of race, gender, color, language, sex, politics, birth place, social origin, status and property. There will be no distinction in respect to one's country's jurisdiction or international status; whether independently, non-self-governing or trust under other sovereignty.

c)   Liberty, security of person and life itself is everyone's right.

d)   Everyone is free from slavery or any form of servitude; the trade of slaves Is a crime in any form.

e)   Everyone is free of any kind of torture to cruel and inhuman acts and treatments

f)   All humans have the right to be recognized as a person by law.

g)   Everyone is equal by law and entitled to be equally protected by the law without any discrimination.

h)   All have equal right to efficient remedy by national tribunals for taking actions that violates the basic rights given to him by the law.

i)   All is free from becoming subjects of arbitrary arrests, exile or detention.

j)   All has equal entitlement to fair and public hearing from both independent tribunal and impartial tribunal, in deciding whether his obligation and any crime charged against him.

k)   All who are charged with a criminal offense are by right, innocent, and should be treated as such before proven guilty by the public trial in which he is guaranteed all necessary defense.

l)   None should let interference of their privacy, home, family or correspondence. There shouldn't be an attack on one's honor either. All have equal right to be protected by law against all kinds of such attack.

m)   Everybody has their rights to move freely and where to reside in state borders. Anybody can leave their country and visit any country.

n)   If persecuted, anyone can seek and enjoy a foreign country's asylum. This right is not invoked when persecutions are genuinely risen in cases that are not politically related.

o)   Everybody has an equal right to have a nationality. No one should be denied tier nationality or changing their nationality.

p)   With no limitations like nationality, race or religion, all ag appropriate men and women have a right to marriage and to build their family. They are guaranteed equal marriage rights during marriage and after its dissolution. Marriage will only be allowed if both parties are willing and none must be forced to their will. Family is naturally the primary group segment of society. It must be protected by state and society.

q)   Everybody can own properties on their own and in relation to others. No one must be deprived of his properties.

r)   Freedom of conscience, and of thoughts, and of religion is given as an equal right to everybody. This includes the freedom to make changes on one's beliefs or religion. And freedom to teach others these beliefs whether in private in public and to make these beliefs into practice of worship and of observation.

s) Everybody is rightfully entitled to freely express themselves and their opinions; whether seeking or receiving information by any media, and without interference.

t) Everybody is entitled to peaceful assembly and association.

u) Everybody is entitled to partake in governing his country, whether directly or by choosing freely, a representative. All has their rights to partake in public services of their country.

v) Everybody who is a member of a social group, has a right to security of society and given freedom to access these securities.

w) Everybody as his freedom to work and choice of employment/career. He must receive a favorable terms/conditions of employment and to be protected against unemployment. Everybody, irrespective of discrimination, must be given equal Wages of labor. All are entitled to become a member of any trade union to protect their own interest.

x) Everybody is entitled to live in their own standards for the well-being of themselves and their family which includes the kinds of food, housing and clothing, medical care and all other social and public services.

y) Everybody is entitled equal rights to education

z) Everybody can freely partake in their community culture and enjoy and share artifacts.

SELF-WILL AND SELF-DISCIPLINE

A self-willed person is one is unmindful of other's will and wishes. More often than not, society sees a self-willed person as unreasonable, dominant or stubborn. They are quite challenging to deal with because of their focus on themselves and their decisions. Their selfishness doesn't come from a greed to put their well-being in first- a self-willed person may be a martyr. However, their selfishness is from an ardent desire to follow what they think is the right path.

The will power of a self-willed person is conscious, determined and exert. This will could be described in 3 main categories:

· **I WILL** this gives one the determination to venture into something without losing interest or giving up. It is what puts a person on a treadmill rather than letting the person stay idle on the couch.

· **I WON'T POWER** this is the power to resist temptation. This power comes to play when on chose not to eat ice-cream and chocolate if the goal is to lose weight.

· **I WANT POWER** it gives a long-term influence of one's decision. It is the power that focus on delay of gratification. The famous experiment carried by Stanford marshmallow shows that people who delay gratification are better off than those with instant gratification.

First thing to consider while identifying a self-willed person;

1   Independence go a long way when becoming self-willed. A person will address issues in a unique and different path. She loves a challenge and she invent new ways to solve them. If they get to a point of needing assistance, they will openly and ask. There is strength in admitting fault. A strong-willed person is not afraid of

other people's thought about him because he only values' his thoughts and opinions.

2   To be self-willed, one must be thoughtful about most things. Their minds are rich with information about almost anything because they are constantly learning about these things. They analyze events on emotions and take sufficient effort to act on it. They are constantly putting puzzle pieces together-in different forms of interest like in businesses or politic, and to make sense of what is going on. They are wildly imaginative they are the creators of extraordinary ideas.

3   They are inquisitive about their surroundings and so they question every rule set by society. It doesn't necessarily mean that they are law breakers, it simply means that they are aware of their human rights. they don't tolerate when they are taken for granted.

4   They are very passionate about their interests. They will go the extreme to achieve their goals and vision because they are not easily afraid of a challenge. They have the fix-it mentality which in most cases, optimistic. They are persistent in their endeavors.

5   They are the most faithful, loyal and trustworthy. Self-willed people have a high moral and they care genuinely for loved ones. They only trust few people so they try to stick with the selected few. These people are truthful and honest and because they believe in their moral conducts, they have no reason to hide them for others opinion.

6   They place high value on their freedom and personal space. A Self-willed person don't like interference when making their own decisions. They need time and space to meditate which involves taking a break from the crowd once in a while. This person trusts his instinct and let their voice lead them.

7   The biggest critic of a strong-willed person is himself. This makes them consistently improving on themselves because they are aware of being better. This owes to the fact they place high self-esteem. They don't hesitate to admit to failure hence they re-strategize to turn failure to success even though it takes a longer time (i.e. the concept of failing forward).

8   A self-willed person says less and do more. They only say what they will do. They are straight forward and direct with their speech. They only speak up after they had gathered their thoughts which gives their words credibility. This means that their choices are often right than none.

Self-willed and strong-willed are one in the same. To become strong-willed, one must first discover self and trust in self. However, a self-willed person must exercise self-discipline in order to maintain a steady mental state.

Mastering self-discipline

A very important skill for leadership is self-discipline. This is essential and effective in daily life and how one deals with events. Although, while everyone acknowledges its power, only few people are experts in exercise it.

What is self-discipline?

It is an inner source of power that fuel's one decision and compels one to follow them thoroughly. It is a control of thought, action and emotions. This is important in all types of leaderships because it enables a leader to stick to decisions without changing minds. It makes perseverance look easy, which indicates a high sense of positivity and self-esteem. A leader knows that he will succeed, therefore puts in will-power. Feelings that are distracting by nature:

addiction, laziness and procrastination, can have no significance in the lives of sufficient self-discipline.

Daily challenges are unavoidable and handling them properly means ensuring that it doesn't upset our health and well-being of both self and the environment. In all type of strategy/tactics in dealing with problems, it is important to exercise patience, persistence and perseverance.

The lack of this skill leads to loss and failure. E.g. a person must have mastered self-discipline in overcoming negative habits like smoking, over-eating, relationship problem, else the person will never achieve goal.

Other Advantages of self-discipline;

- It lets one not to act on impulse
- It helps to fulfil promises made to self and others
- It overcomes procrastination
- It gives extra drive even after the initial rush of enthusiasm to start a project
- It wakes one early so to utilize the limited hours of the day.

CHAPTER THREE
QUEST FOR BALANCE BETWEEN FREEDOM AND DISCIPLINE

S ocial judgement is an effect of choice made by a person or group of people. Sociability or warmth, are the fundamental perspective of any organization social judgement. Each choice has its reward, referred to as reward or repercussion.

The mechanism of deciding whether a choice is worth making the mind is constantly measuring action and its reactions. e.g. knowing when to quit hitting snooze on the alarm clock and get out of bird early to prepare for the morning and the hours that follow. Also knowing when to turn of the Television for bed-time at night.

Clinical mechanism of deciding whether a choice is worth making

The mind is constantly measuring action and its reactions. e.g. knowing when to quit hitting snooze on the alarm clock and get out of bird early to prepare for the morning and the hours that follow. Also knowing when to turn of the Television for bed-time at night.

According to a new research carried out by Emory university psychologist, the brain's ventromedial cortex which previously was declared insignificant in strong-willed choices, now appears as the most vital role. It is responsible for the formation of "what to expect" when taking decisions and making choices. A human brain normally functions when considering decisions and the efforts that will support decision making. It provides ways to clarify a disorder of reduced motivations such in cases of schizophrenia or depression.

There are 3 brain segments of the brain in making decisions.

1.   The Anterior Insula (al)

2.   The ventromedial prefrontal cortex (vmPFC)

3.   The Dorsal Anterior cingulate cortex dACC)

Studies described the vmPFC as central computation of a person's value during making a decision. However, the subject of 'effort' to be spent, those values are not analyzed by the vmPFC but rather by the other 2 brain segments.

Real world problems urge most people, if not all, to make choices that are based on incomplete data. A study designed by Arulpragasam was carried by model of distinct neural analysis and computation for the rewards and effort of human choices. The subject went through FMRI while making decisions that required efforts. It was found that he cost on effort and it reword on 'choice' were separated in time.

The subject will make little or no effort on decision making and earn $1, or make significant effort and the monetary exchange will be increased to a significant $5. How this is measured in this experimental study made by Arulpragasam was by involving rapid buttons for each participant.

In the first trial, the participants in this research were given the result, represented by a vertical bar with percentages of each button pressing rate. The researcher then informed them that there will be a reward for pressing the buttons when they are making decisions.

After the participants understood what's at stake for the paid experiment, the result showed clearly the role of vmPFC was encoding when expecting an information. The result also showed that dACC and AI are also involved when encoding the different participants on what they earned rather than the effort they put into earning.

Popular debate argues that there is a separate neural circuit on making the effort for decisions that are affected by risks and probabilities. Nevertheless, all the three segments of the brain are in work, only that in different ways when a person measures and undertake efforts in decision making.

The diagram below represents the 7 stages in decision making:

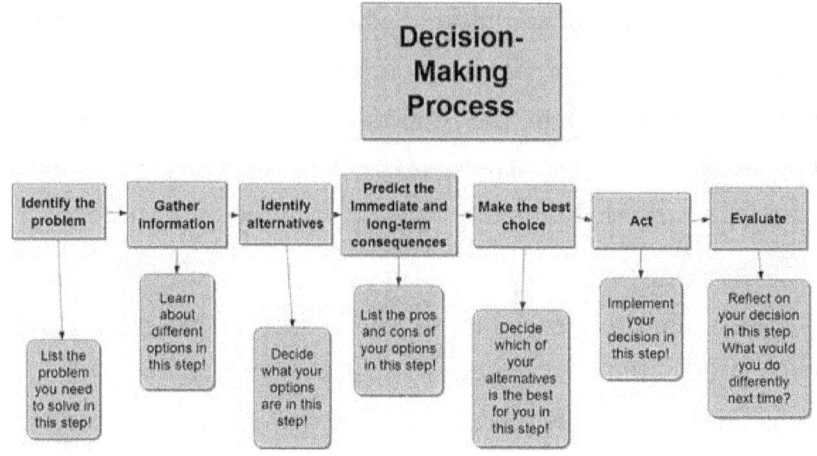

Having an initiative to do something is one step ahead then follows the 7 other steps. Without planning and undergoing a strategic thinking, choices can never be made. Why do people plan a project well but fail to plan the decision-making process?

One must first decide that there is a decision to be made, it begins the process. It is different from having initiative because there is effort in coming to a conclusion. This is obvious right? But most people and even corporations are guilty of indecisiveness. The worst is when ignorant of what issue must be attended to. It not only cause issues complications, (i.e increasing damages and consequences)

It's important to be sure and be specific in taking this step. Another challenge faced by most people when taking this step is that they make vague images of problems. This is an example of why leaders must be self-disciplined when making goals and be non-emotional about pinning issues. Lack of not pinning the issue lets decision to miss its target.

The next step is to collect information. A well-informed decision makes higher impressions and effects. What is the critical data needed on that subject? also take into consideration end result: End results could be internal and external. It could be both in very good days one is in the maximum productivity threshold. It also includes the media to source for this information. i.e. both mental and physical way of dealing with a problem. When a media is in line with the problem, the accuracy in predicting what the issue is greater than when the data is false and not inline. In this stage of process, leaders seek advice from the organization. Note that family is the first social institution that a person experience.

Also note that there are many ways to acquire information on a subject. For example, two sisters, Mary and Martha had different personalities. Mary was tall and slender than Martha. Mary was more active in physically demanding activities. Martha liked exercising in a more theatrical style in drama class. The differences also reflect well in each girl's approach to a challenge. And in the media whether Books or the Internet.

At this point, one has acquired a bunch of information about the problem and a number of solutions. it's good to have as many solutions. experiment to dilute to the best fit. This process is simply described as Task-gathering process. It's not yet time to decide, leaders must take time to practice these intuitions. That's why leaders are creative and self-willed. The freedom to explore new territories allow people to express themselves.

What a person will like to do at this time is to give value to the decision. That means judging evidence.

It means being the attorney of all sides and to be so, one must learn to master emotions. Ask what is the repercussion of embarking on the goal. Most people will fall short in procrastination because misplaced values to get a task done. A self-willed person trusts their instincts. they have a strong opinion about what is right and wrong. To have self-control means appreciating values.

The 5th stage is about making a choice-The Choice. It's now to take a decision after passing through the experimental phase of ideas. It's now time to pick one and stick to it. Note that this doesn't involve taking action yet. The mind and emotions must be ready and set before the body follows. This is why leaders needs to discipline their emotions in order to exercise self-control. This is usually the most difficult stage to deal with because there is nothing tangible to measure yet. The previous step where more cerebral exercise so there was nothing at stake. Now for the first time in this process, change is about to be exert.

The next stage is the action phase. No more excuses and procrastination. No more information gathering or studying the odds. It's time to act. The tragedy is when most people spend all their time calculating the odds and recalculating strategy. It could last a lifetime. However, a leader must take that first step into physically changing/solving the problem. An employer doesn't hire a professional to think, he must act as well and fast. The main work is done- acquiring the data. Now it's time to apply it. Now all the instincts and gut feeling are pointing towards one direction-Implementation. But take note to not implement blindly. Be careful when acting, (i.e. be observant and also study reactions). Information gathering is never ending.

Every decision is a teaching moment. Taking time to analyze each decision made and if it worked (or not) and study consequences of actions. Study the results. had the decision worked as planned? Measure whether the right choice was made through the previous decision steps. A person will know if his decision proved effective.

If it didn't, then it could be that the problem was not clearly defined or error owing to the other stages of decision making.

A leader never worries in this stage because she knows it's not the end of the world- it's also another opportunity to improve plan and work on the problem. He/she knows is aware that this stage is unavoidable (as in failing forwards), sometimes plan works and other times it doesn't, but it's unnecessary to beat self about it. Most people will get angry or depressed in this stage, at the end of the decision if it doesn't go as planned. A leader knows not to give up. Rather explore why it hasn't gone the way it was planned. Decision process isn't perfect. Now that the result is analyzed, take a different angle towards talking the problem. Let the second approach be different from the first. One main problem with many of us is that we don't like change. It's important not to be clingy to one leadership tactic. Just because it solved one problem doesn't guarantee it will solve the next.

Nature vs Nurture

The popular debate about nature versus nurture involves to what extent in which behaviors in humans and animals affect the inherited like genetics or acquired traits like in learning and how these are being influenced.

Nature, in this book, will be described as whatever we think as already wired which is influenced by biological factors. Whereas, nurture are the external/environmental factors, e.g., life experiences, a result of exposure and learning about an individual.

This popular debate, nature-nurture, is mostly concerned about the effect it has on a human behavior like a person's personality, her cognitive characteristics, psychopathology and her temperament.

Approaches to Psychology

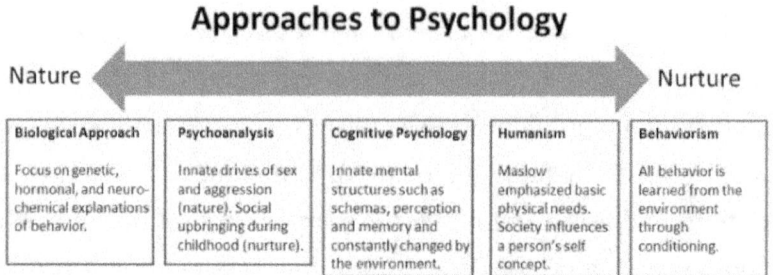

It is well known that some physical traits are commonly formed from biological traits which is generic. A person's features like eye color, hair texture, skin pigmentation, and some diseases such as Huntingdon chorea, are all biologically determined and hereditary.

These is what triggers another popular debate about Leaders being born or if made. Meaning that characteristics of a person's psych, such as personality, mental capacity or behavioral attributes are pre-wired before a person is born.

Nativist is a term given to those who believe extremely about hereditary and its complete influence on a person. The basis of their believes centers around that the human species is a product of centurial evolution and conflict/differences are evidence of an individual unique genes. In measuring the degree of heredity traits, *Heritability* is the term given to describe, whether or not an individual has a high heritability or low heritability.

An example of high heritability is in the case of Chomsky, year 1965. That proposed speaking of different languages. It was speculated that language is gained by innate acquisition code of humans. Freud's theory is another great example of nature position, that aggression is an innate drive referred to as Thanatos.

Maturity is an essential term used in nature position which describes how a person's differences and characteristics are not noticeable by birth and only emerge in time. This means that everybody has an inner natural or biological timer which activates on and off- already programmed. Example of this phenomenon is in puberty. The nativists will argue the reason of maturity is what controls mental development, language fluency and infant's attachments.

Unlike *Naturism* owing to extreme natural influences, *Empiricism* are purely environmental inclined. Owing human characteristics to external effects. Their assumption is that an individual's mind from birth is a blank space and only begins to fill in time through experiences.

At the point where the individual develops mental characteristics, it now called Learning (as opposed to maturing). "How one is brought up" is now the basis and reason for one's developmental stages in behavior and mental capacity.

An example of this concept applies in Bandura social learning study. Stating that aggression is learned from observation and environmental imitations. Skinner studies also proposed that learning a language is a result of other people in our environment.

Also, Freud's theory states that event from our childhood shapes our characteristics/personalities in adulthood. His theory stresses the importance of parents and why to take care in bringing up a child. Here, family is an important social group. This concept, the environmentalist theory, was predominant in the 20th century in psychology.

Today, there are hardly anyone who accepts either of this extreme theory. There is too many credibility on both sides. Rather than ask

"Which is?" being influenced in a particular situation (Nature or Nurture) is better to ask "how much?" is being influenced. This is important in decision making because there are some factors that cannot be changed, e.g., weather, but can affect the plan/outcome of decision, e.g. Planning a family picnic on a rainy day.

This means that both hereditary traits and environmental influence are both affecting an individual's daily life. Which is more important?

A famous 19th century relative of Charles Darwin, Francis Galton, was sure that intellectuals where the result of intelligent ancestral genes. He was convinced about the product of a natural superiority.

This believe has stipulated many researches into intelligence test. One of such tests by psychologist, Arthur Jenson. In his test, he found ta black American average IQ score is significantly lower than white Americans, arguing about the credibility and responsibilities of genes. He stated that the overall intelligence factor takes up 80% genetics.

Surprisingly, this created controversies more in social and political issues than in the main work itself. America storm at the time of this Jenson's publication wasn't due to empirical and its logic. Galton also suggested that society will be better off with better breeding. American eugenic Society in America, 1920, campaigned for sterilization of people in psychiatric hospital. Many people believe that immigration is created to discriminate Asians and black ethnicity.

Environmentalist will view the same IQ scores and base the result to part inbuilt testing methods. There believes are different mental and intellectual strengths are due to social qualities(inequalities) placed on material acquisitions i.e. resources and opportunities. They will argue, living in a ghetto will tend a lower score than a privileged society member- dominated by white ethnicity.

This is why the nature-nurture argument will stand the test of time because its core beliefs are both cross-sessional. What is an attempt to understand from a nature perspective will up structs a society issue-This debate cuts across gender differences where controversies about how much? is owed to behavior in respect to genetics and exposure.

Behavioral genetic research shows that there are behavior changes that are affected by genetics known as hereditary units that passed down to generations. Psychologist can now measure in quantity, the of attributes that owes to nature or nurture through specific characteristics and mental traits. A way this can be easily experimented is comparing a group that shares a common gene(nature) and in their different environment/ community(nurture). A natural way this may be carried out is by adoption.

Studies have shown that most kids adopted by foster parents resembles their biological parents. This oppose the environmental concept of behavior. Another way to view hereditary concept as an advantage over environmental concept is in birth of twins who are either identical (share the same gene) or not (only 50% shared genes). It proves that psychological characteristics is extremely determined by hereditary.

Polygenic inheritance focus on focus on the multiplicity of genetics that a person inherits rather than one single gene in a slightly different perspective. Behavior psychologists demonstrates how thousands of genetics are encoded collectively which contributes to identity (personalities and behaviors). Depression can be seen as a mental state affected by polygenic that follows being influenced by thousands of genes.

Moral Dilemma

Nurture, sometimes will correspond to both psychological and environmental outcomes of a person. E.g. how well parents read books to their children and how often that children know how to read are relative to determining the outcome of a child's mental ability to read. Here, behavior psychologist admits that most times, what may be referred to as environmental ideas are actually a mirror to a person's genetic uniqueness. People are what builds society and communities. They create and modify their environment via emotional and mental toleration. This simply means that what looks like nature may be simply nurtured devised and vice versa.

Recently, questions about *how much* environmental influence a person or how it is affected by genetic characteristics has become unresolvable. However, psychologist is beginning to speculate that the wrong questions are being asked concerning this subject. In reference to intelligence quota, there are many factors to consider in measurement. It is due to a complex phenomenon which reveal intelligence in many types of ways. "how much" quantifies a person's behavior characteristics and personality traits in numeric values. Genetic and nongenetic attributes have been proven to work together to build a person. In daily life, how a person approach is greatly determined by both genes i.e. temperament and strategic position of strength. Goals are achieved by examining and mastering both factors.

Rather than lead on either of the two extreme ideas about nature or nurture, it is better to study how the two concepts interact with each other. This means subscribing to the fact that a person's mental state, either developed or disordered are influenced to a great degree by genetic predisposition and community. It now makes better sense to describe why and why people behave differently.

A research on human genome stimulates a great interest in tracing the different type of behavior via specific DNA strands which is located in the chromosome. It is an advanced study of how genetic behavior. When applying these two concepts to solve an issue, the chances of decision making will increase. This makes it possible lean self-disciple through knowing how to control emotions. By asking this question "why do I feel this way", one can quickly identify the issue- starting the first stage of decision-making.

CHAPTER FOUR
EMPATHY AND
COMMUNICATION

Moral Dilemma Cont.

Imagine a scenario where you are taking a walk to the shop with your best friend Diana. Diana informs you that a classmate, Christy, stole some money at the school's cafeteria. Unfortunately, Christy blamed Diana for the theft and Diana was suspended for 2 weeks until she pays back the money that Christy stole.

As you both enter the shop, you see Christy. Diana pushes Christy slightly and Christy does the same. Unknown to Christy, Diana had slipped a pair of earrings into Christy's purse and just as Christy was about leaving the shop, the alarm goes off and she is pulled aside by security. Christy says she is innocent and blames Diana for the misunderstanding but Diana, your best friend, claims to have nothing to do with the scene and asked for your support.

Your options are:

A.   tell the truth- if so, Diana will be revealed as the culprit to the crime, she will get into trouble again and face the repercussions from both her parents and the law. Christy will go free and not face any repercussions for originally stealing from the school cafeteria.

B.   Tell a lie to back Diana up- if so, Christy will face the repercussion of shoplifting from the store and your best friend will finally be avenged. However, will have committed a serious crime by lying to the police officer and Christy's punishment would be more severe than her original crime measures.

Now the police come to you and ask for what happened, what will you tell them?

'Moral dilemma' is popularly used interchangeably with 'ethical dilemma'. This means that most moral cases are to a large degree, similar to ethical codes. Moral or ethical dilemmas are situations where a person must choose between or more actions which presents itself as morally unacceptable, whether real life situations or imaginations.

Moral dilemma is a thought-provoking imaginative experiment that is employed to compare philosophical credibility in decision making. They present themselves as an ethical system so that if one argues that a philosophy is unreasonable, it means that the entire ethical system may be incomplete.

Although, the conditions of moral/ethical dilemma in its right, is a major topic of philosophical debate. Some philosophers strongly argue that moral dilemma doesn't exist, that decisions take a form of being either black or white. While others will argue that moral dilemma exist and are unavoidable but do not actually represent the ethical system is flawed. Therefore, moral dilemma is an avenue to explore what the ethical system must accomplish and what it shouldn't accomplish in individuality and society.

To state plainly, moral dilemmas is just another tool to explore personal values. It is neither wrong nor right. It varies from person to person and in groups to other groups. "what will you tell them?" this question will as be opposed to "what is the truth" in the case of implicating either Diana or Christy. Moral dilemma will reveal a person's priority or urge a person to decide what their priority is.

Many moral dilemmas are a result of conflict between deontological (what is right) and teleological (what result is good). However, there are some moral dilemmas that arise which is independent of this two but rather take a more systematic issue- when they require making a choice from closely related option, e.g. saving only one life out of two lives, both innocent.

The Origin

Historically, the first ever moral dilemma that is in record is written in the bible. Then, Abraham experienced a moral dilemma when he was asked by God to sacrifice his only son, Isaac. The options were either to murder his beloved and only son from Sarah, or face the repercussion of disobeying almighty God. Nevertheless, the story of Abraham ought to have been before Moses implemented the 10 commandments, it seems that people at that era would consider both obeying God and murdering their son. This story illustrates the significance of obedience and its values, therefore promotes deontological ethical system (based on a standard rule not result).

Another historical records of moral dilemma can be seen in ancient Greeks philosophy when Socrates made an argument against Plato's claims in Republic. The Republic demonstrates equality in speaking the truth and paying one's debt while Socrates identified the unreliability of the stated ethical codes. Socrates pointed out that there has been some error a case of paying/returning kinds of debt, e.g. a gun that was borrowed from a friend who isn't in his right mind shouldn't be returned else, the lender may be prone to violence. It seems as though this great philosopher was just being too difficult here, but he was only trying to make a point by moral dilemmas. He also pointed on the same case that ethical rules have its relative priorities. i.e. there are two different priorities to consider here: the first is doing one's best to prevent harm of self and others and the second priority that may be noticed here is the ethic of repaying debt/loan. Which will you choose? This is a popular example of moral dilemma which urges a n ethical system to instill priority and values on its rules. The truth is that prioritizing values depends greatly in the condition that presents itself. Afterall, both options are ethically right.

Over the recent years, society has seen many real dilemmas becoming political and social issues. These dilemmas are increasingly demanding in cases of abortion and death penalty. A person's opinion on this issue depends mainly on a person's value. What will it be: protect a life or take a life?

There will be more ethical dilemma that will arise in the future that relates to science and technological advancements. Moral Dilemma seems to be an unavoidable issue because as the world keeps changing and reforming, priorities changes as well. It is good to keep in mind that in daily life, priorities may change and while it does, we shouldn't cling to tasks that used to be on the top of our TO-DO list but isn't as important anymore.

It is advisable that each day, we should review our list of priorities and have a clear value in reaching that goal.

C³ Principal- Criticism, Condemnation and Complaint

"Any fool can criticize, complain and condemn- and most fools do. It takes character to be understanding and forgiving" _ Dale Carnegie

A book written by renowned author and orator, Dale Carnegie, How to Win Friends and Influence people, revealed the significance of Criticizing, condemning and complaining about people. Knowing the gravity of the 3 Cs will go a long way in daily life situations in how to deal with people.

The first principle in Carnegie's work known as the first Law- **DON'T** criticize, condemn and complain about people or in fact, anything at all. If a case arises and its needed to do so, it's better to pass the message in a healthier way. Communication goes a great length in leadership and for communication to properly take place, a person needs to understand Empathy.

Leadership is majorly about leading – and a leader must have followers to lead. To influence others to follow a course, it's important to learn how to compel and influence people. If not, people will go on the defense and no message will be successfully communicated. They will bring up million reasons not to follow the course and shortly begin to avoid the person who doesn't know how to speak to them. This is because people naturally adopt the mirror concept that blame external factors for their mistakes rather than looking inwards. They interpret the criticism as an attack on their pride and personality which triggers resentment.

It's important to remember that dealing with people means to be in communion with irrational beings, unlike when dealing with computers that require logic. People have emotions affected by prejudice and motivated by vanity. Great leaders recognize that this is a natural flaw and they don't bother to change it but to work with it to their benefits.

Most times when people make mistakes, we view it as an irrational decision but by seeing that mistake, the action, from a completely different point of view, we may soon understand why the action was taken in the first place. This is what it means to exercise empathy. In the time that Abraham Lincoln's spouse spoke in Illy about southern American people, Abraham Lincoln's responded by telling her that its fair not to criticize them because he and she may have done the same under the same conditions. What Lincoln meant was that we all have our morals that is built from our values and personal experiences, so its unwise to think that our moral is superior than others.

It is what popular lessons will state; one man's meat is another man's poison. What may seem as a crazy irrational behavior to one person may be rational and logical to the other. This is can be explained for the various behaviors than the human race exhibit. A leader knows that by criticizing a behavior that might seem irrational to him, the result will be reciprocated criticism rather than change.

Even when dealing with a logical individual that prides himself for being accountable for his mistake, criticizing, condemning and complaining about his flaws will also rigger resentment. This so-called reasonable individual is the ultimate critic of himself, so when an external voice tells him of his shortcomings, he will decode the message as an insult to his injury.

A popular behavior psychologist named BF Skinner, found out that animals responds better when they are rewarded or given a threat for being well behaved rather than punished for bad behaviors. Apparently, humans respond in the same way. We like to hear our better qualities and know how to improve on them as opposed to our "bad qualities" that needs changing. It always feels better to discuss positive/uplifting reinforcement than the feeling of being scolded for someone else judgement.

A leader knows that mistakes are unavoidable. Even in decision making, mistakes are bound to happen. All famous leaders experienced failure in more than one way and in different situations. Their mistakes didn't make them any less great. When a person knows that their mistakes wouldn't be deemed as stupidity or any other negative comments but rather threatened in leeway, she will be more open to improvement with an elevated spirit.

Consider a loss as a lesson. This approach Is a great way of dealing with emotions especially in unexpected scenarios. People experience emotional breakdowns because they have either been too hard on themselves or on someone else. A person is mentally healthy that sees a problem from a neutral perspective (i.e. stripped off prejudice) so when mistakes arise, they are emotionally stable. Therefore, seeing faults insensitively and correcting the mistake. If a person is humiliated for an inevitable mistake, he/she is more likely to quit.

Bob hoover story, a popular pilot, was mentioned in Dale Carnegie's book. The pilot was on a flight that had an engine malfunction. Two of the engines stopped working. He successfully and miraculously maneuvered the plane to crash land, though the plain got destroyed but the passengers and his crew were unscratched.

When Hoover inspected the plane after the crash, he discovered that the engines weren't fueled with the appropriate gasoline but rather jet fuel. A critical mistake. When hoover returned to the station, he asked for the mechanic responsible for servicing the plane. Hoover was so angry because that cash would have cost lives, he could have teared the mechanic apart. Surprisingly, he retaliated by grabbing the mechanic's shoulders, who was already weeping and said "to show that I'm certain you will never repeat this mistake again, I will have you service F-51 by tomorrow"

It's better to seek and understand why people make mistakes rather than scolding destructively even though justified. In that way, one can learn from their mistakes without having to experience it. It is a great way to study and examine our surroundings and the people around. It always feels better to forgive and move forward.

Negotiation and Compromise

There are 4 basic strategies of a principled negotiation:

1. <u>First strategy</u>- Not Personalities but Issue

   In all negotiations, all parties involved have a substantial interest in the subject and relationships amongst themselves. Meaning that when negotiating, it is important to consider the object that demands negotiation and the relationship of the people negotiating. A position bargain prioritizes the object above relationships. In a principled negotiation, it is important to preserve the relationships of the people and the object. It can be simple done by

   - Identifying different perception to view the object

   - Proposing a well-structured plan so that the other party doesn't "lose face"

   - Accepting emotions that will surface during the course of negotiating and dealing with them accordingly.

- Exercising great communication skills through attentive listening and comprehensive speaking.

2. Second Strategy- Breaking free of Position Negotiation trap:

   This can be done in 4 simple ways when identifying interest

   - Ask the obvious question. Why has the other party refused your proposal and why have you refused theirs? The common answer is that the interest benefits the opposing party or the opposing party feels that the interest is biased.

   - Talk more about Interests. This will enable a better communication and clear conscience.

   - While interests are revealed, keep records.

   - Ensure to acknowledge the other party's interest as credible and refrain from criticizing.

3. Third Strategy- Seek a WIN-WIN outcome

   Most cases, the reason why people detest negotiation as a communication tool is that most people approach the object from a positional bargain. Therefore, leaving the involved parties with destructive emotions. Most people experience Loser-Winner relationships. The problem is that positional negotiation is a win or lose game- all or nothing. It doesn't promote a healthy relationship amongst the people involved, the price is only in the interest of the object. Most cases, the losing party is bitter and nurture resentment which is an unhealthy state of mind. It is a very competitive and stressful game for even the winners in this kind of game. Leaders exercise creativity when approaching negotiations. To them, there is no loser so they try possible best to create an avenue that legitimates and keeps all party's interest.

For example, in the case of a bank who loan money to a business for a collateral that is valued at fairly the same amount. When the borrower defaults in payment, the bank has an option of either granting more time to repay or seizing the property. If the bank takes a positional angle, it will retrieve its money's worth and risk a bitter customer who has probably become homeless, else it could approach from a WIN-WIN situation and get its money worth in a stretched time. This way, the bank may construct other means of payment methods while preserving a customer's home and health.

4. <u>Fourth Strategy</u>- objective Stands

This means stating out facts because different interests, needs and opinions most likely affect people's interpretation of facts. It causes people to subscribe to the fact that only supports their interests and position.

The magic secret to keeping a good and lasting relationship is the act of compromise. It means giving up on one's needs and realizing that nobody is perfect so that every relationship requires a bit of a give and take. Sadly, in due time, the one who compromise will feel cheated and taken for granted.

However, genuine compromise is intended to gain a precise angle. It is the middle ground for all parties involved. For 2 partners, it means half way the line-50%. Usually it forms from passivity which is a reaction when reaching a roadblock (dead-end to achieving 100% interest), therefore, if not handled carefully, it may produce emotional results of a positional negotiation since it's out of control.

In reality, nobody completely gets their way. Compromise is usually justified by observations, results and assumptions of the object's interests. Both parties' earlier campaign for "My way vs Your way" and at a point either of the parties will give up and subscribe partly to the other's interest. It is an exhausting cycle. For example, when one's partner doesn't call as often as one would like them to, one will grumble over it in secrecy in fear of speaking out and causing an issue. Eventually, one will simply accept that behavior and live with it- this is compromising.

Instead of compromising, why not negotiate the terms of the relationship? Will you like your partner to call every day or rather once a week? Negotiation is important to begin any relationship; it keeps a clear view of what is at stake while reaching the goal. It prioritizes values, whether objectively or people. In the case of a partner calling either every day or once a week, negotiation may result to calling 3 times a week.

Note that negotiation may also involve compromises, but in the case of passively compromising which pent-up emotions, active compromise is more intentional. It is consciously being aware and taking decision of interest- walking to the middle ground on your own.

Many people get emotionally overwhelmed because they feel out of control about their conditions. In real life situations may arise which demands critical thoughts and approaches, especially in dealing with people. Leaders have mastered the art of communication. They creatively device WIN-WIN deals in which helps them get ahead in line. They are able to communicate effectively by knowing the other parties' interest and convincing them to come to a common ground. A good leader must be a great listener, else, he may not understand what the other person wants.

Often times, people don't even know what they want. They may claim to need one thing, but really, it's something else that they need. Leaders are able to read between the lines. This is achievable by studying what the person isn't saying, like body movement, facial expression, hand gestures etc.

CHAPTER FIVE
HOW TO ATTAIN FREEDOM BY DISCIPLINE

It easy to believe that going with one's flow means freedom-Not being subjected by any circumstance, being able to freely change mind at any time. But on the contrary, real freedom is a self-discipline and self-control. If the goal is creating something, you notice that the growth and development stage demands the use of self-discipline. It demands constant attention, nurturing and action. It demands that an individual understand how his mind works and working with the mind.

Self-discipline are set of skills and strategy which puts and individual in the driver's seat of both mind and emotion so that he can take absolute power over his subconsciousness. It's a self-taught process to follow directions about who we really want to be in life. Everything comes with a manual- first law of motion states that an action always produce an equal and opposite reaction and self-discipline enables how to properly make the required action. Humans are a walking habit machine, it's a pre-coded characteristic. We are also wired to react in a specific way to a specific actions and performance. This is fact. With self-discipline, we consciously choose the reaction of our action- That's what freedom is choosing the outcome of your life.

Just as self-discipline is a creation mechanics, it may also serve as a prevention mechanism as well. It keeps and maintain things that can degrade if proper care isn't given, e.g. health and learning, and it prevents small issues from escalating.

"Yes, you need to do the work. You need to put in the hours, the day, the week, the month, and the years. You need to get on the path and stay on the path- the path that leads to the positive transformations, as the path leads to a better you, the path leads to freedom" _ Jocko Willink

Significance of self-discipline in daily life

Aside from the fact that freedom is a proven result of self-discipline, there are a number of other benefits that can be noticeable in a person's life which owes its true meaning to Self-Love.

I.   A person functions in partnership with self, whereby self is a representation of one's true nature and personality. It takes self-love to accept your biological and mental design and work with it.

II. Person is kinder to self by given what's best and avoiding what is not.

III.A person develops trust for self because self-discipline requires commitment which builds self-reliance.

IV. A person becomes confidence. This is due to self-trust/reliance. When a person begins to rely on themselves and trust their efforts, they develop a sense of comfort and confidence because they know that they can get anything they want. All it will take is trusting myself to put in the work.

V. A person is happier because they know that they are the boss of themselves. They can control the waves of temptation by choosing when to be passive and aggressive with instant gratification. A self-disciplined person isn't conflicted inwardly about what to do. They know, understand, and comply with the gravity of their actions.

VI. A person finds ability to complete projects even after the initial drive/enthusiasm has faded. Self-discipline assures a person that the end is inevitably a reward.

VII . A person is free of guilt and judgement. One's biggest critic is one's self. With self-disciple, one can stop beating themselves about what to do because one already knows. Instead. The negative energy that comes with self-doubt is converted to positive energy that rewards a person for hat is done so far.

VIII. A person becomes a master of his time because discipline requires working with time. To achieve any goal requires settling deadline. The problem that arise from setting a goal without time frame of reaching that goal is Procrastination.

IX . A person feels good about themselves and that is what keeps a good relationship with others. Everybody loves to be around positive energy and self-loved people.

Of course, a lot can be accomplished by practicing self-discipline with higher consciousness and consistency. All self-discipline that is practiced is actually self-love in play and this single knowledge changes the attitude of practicing self-mastery. It doesn't necessarily need to be a rigid attitude of organizing one's daily life, maybe in the beginning, but in a short time, it flows easily.

Discipline is what makes whatever we feed our mind to manifest. It is what makes dreams come true. Creation and manifestation are the essence of what gives meaning to our life. Limitations contains upward movement/growth. We limit our mind by staying in the safe zone which doesn't require any effort or discomfort. Change and evolution occurs when outside the comfort zone. It is impossible to transform when still clinging to old habits which are responsible for a false sense of safety and security. it's just as it is, to create a different result needs a different action else, act the same and remain in that one spot.

However, don't make the mistake of pushing yourself too hard. That isn't self-love, in that case, you run the risk a rebel between mind and body which is emotionally unhealthy and takes you 2 steps backwards in accomplishing anything. Instead, make simple and gradual changes for a start. Let the body get used to the change process and have the mind set at the price. The result of keeping body and mind aligned in any growth process is magically transformational.

So, in this sense, freedom to a vague extend is managing boundaries and limitations. For example, reckless spending inevitably leads to scarcity and bankruptcy. However, assuming a person spends on a reasonable budget (in respect to income), it will lead to a life of financial freedom. the same goes for the case of dinking without limitations, the result is a hangover- headache, nausea and no energy the next day. But compared to when drinking in a nice spot in town and a moderate quantity, the experience is quite enjoyable without being troubled by hangover the next day.

Often times, people shun the word 'self-discipline' because it represents the ugly truth- hard work and perseverance as key to success. The leaders are those who subscribe to this power plan after being aware of its demanding attention. They know that discipline is the quickest way to freedom and they try relentlessly to acquire its mastery. The truth is that it's not easy to exercise self-discipline but it is worth the effort and the price to realizing divine freedom.

But what happens when discipline isn't resulting to freedom?

The spirit will rebel when discipline takes a dense and rigid procedure in daily life. It now becomes to look like a punishment rather than a heartfelt sacrifice in one's course. Discipline ought to be an individual's choice, therefore, it is an action that shouldn't feel forced upon. If not then it becomes a meaningless sacrifice. If discipline take a form of forceful actions, it begins by trying to practice a rigid set of rules, failing at adopting the rules easily into daily life and finally opting out and settling for less result which always feels like a dream kill. This is why full-hearted subscription into discipline must be present so that one doesn't easily give up just because they can. Healthy discipline permits room for breathing, relaxation and expression of self. In this sense, living in bondage is described as finding self in uninfluenced circumstances.

The key in perfecting self-discipline is to make it not seem as if walking on a tight robe with strict guidelines. Imagine working in an organization where everybody is always edgy and unfriendly, at the end of the day, a worker will be mentally dissatisfied because lack of genuinely expressing himself. It's better he intentionally wants to be edgy on his accord because he knows that he needs to be serious at the moment of working and not because the boss said so.

Leaders are able to distinguish between holding on to a tight set of rules that produce high productivity and rules that although, promises a specific result, requires 100% energy. The secret is knowing one's ability and capacity. Only venture into anything when ready. It is unwise to begin a task if you aren't equipped sufficiently. This doesn't imply in only material things like finance or skills, it has to do more with a mental state of mind. When there is too much control, management or order of one's feelings/actions, it produces an unhealthy result- the goal may be achieved but it wouldn't be duly appreciated. Its best to loosen the robe a little and let go of the expectations of "good result" and "bad result", and just hope for the best outcome. Afterall, decision making is a learning process. Let it take the form of failing forward.

How Feelings and Desire Guides Actions

When a person takes the effort to inquire about how she wants to really feel, an opportunity of connecting and engaging with self-arises, which is a very good feeling. There is an inner source of power knowing how you want to feel by an action. This is easily achievable by organizing your day with tasks/rituals. Then allow your desired emotions take charge and fuel up your commitments. It is a subconscious act that measures the extent of wanting something.

Exercise:

1.   Think of something you desperately desire. How much do you want it?

2.   That much? Write it down and feel yourself already having that you really desire.

3.   What did you feel while writing your desires? Write it down as well

4.   Now think of the effort needed to reaching your desire. Compare the feelings of acquiring your desire and how you feel about the work to getting it.

The result will reveal how much you really want to accomplish a goal. If you don't want it that much, it's advisable to redirect your time and energy towards something else that you truly want.

Letting desire to inspire commitment is a good way to keep track on duties. It is less stressful and more interesting when our feelings are involved in accomplishing any goal. The task becomes filled with passion and stripped off any resistivity on workflow. Let specific rituals/tasks vary daily in accordance to one's mood, but let it be in a way that honors the overall goal.

Good Instincts-Bad Instincts

It is encouraged to have a healthy skepticism about "right feelings". Sometimes, things that feels like the 'right' thing to do are usually the wrong things to do. An urge/impulse is a result of a developed brain responding to specific behaviors that has been encoded since the beginning of the human species. This feeling can be categorized as instincts of approachable or avoidable behaviors. What is referred to as approachable instinct is activated by a limbic system/activity which comprise of the nucleus acumens and the ventral tegmental region.

This is a region of the brain that rewards evolutionary behaviors, increasing survival abilities and transmission of genes in aspects of a person's feeding behavior and sexual behavior. There will be an increase(substantially) in dopamine degree when these brain areas are triggered which results in a high level of pleasure. Basically, everything that feels enjoyable (e.g. sunset and chocolate) is often a result of that brain area being active.

This limbic system includes amygdala and the cortex. The amygdala is focused on the avoidance behaviors (fight or flight): mostly flight instincts in a case of danger. It increases the chances of survival. In fact, when a feeling of fear, discomfort, distrust, anger or anxiety overwhelms a person, it is because this region of the brain senses that the object that triggered those feelings is perceived as dangerous. The person feels extremely uncomfortable and decides to get away. This instinct is usually present as a stomach upset or a traction in the throat. It is a somatic anxiety without obvious reason which makes a person to behave in ways that are unusual and counterproductive. It causes a person to avoid things that ought to be approachable.

This center of the brain that triggers fight-flight isn't only affected by environmental factors. Our ideas, thoughts and memories also play a major factor. Consequently, our behaviors are modified to what we 'feel' is pleasant and unpleasant. This is an ineffective form of exercising instincts for the modern man. Imagine this instinct as a software bug in modern programming.

Nevertheless, the human species has an amazingly high amount of functioning capacity and ability. The cortex and its cerebral regions develop complex comprehension about our surroundings. A most impressive ability of human beings is the ability to of mastery and specialization. It is achieved from the hours spent in practicing a specific task which leads to one becoming an expert in that task. It leads a person to perform with incredible ease and a supernaturally without having a conscious mind.

The words 'expertise' and 'experience' is usually misused and misunderstood. Having an experience in a task doesn't necessarily mean having expertise in that particular task. Expertise requires Mastery and for one to be a master in a field means haven spent 10,000 hours of practice. However, the process of spending that time is called experience. To become an expert, one must be experienced but it not vice versa. To have a superhuman 'instinct' about doing something, one must have already put in the work of specialization and expertise. It requires discipline and dedication. A 'gut-feeling' is only true after years of acquired skill on a specific subject. This is why most people believe that learning stops in a person's early twenties(university) because real-life issues arise in late 20s and onwards, where a person is required to implement what has already been learnt- consistent actions becomes a habit.

Reaching mastery and specialization is a great feeling of accomplishment. Experts are genuinely self-disciplined. They accomplish goals with ease which promotes a healthy mentality and emotional capacity. This effort can be seen in talented actors and musicians, athletes, and surgeons. A person who is an expert performs complicated tasks with an incredible ease, elegance and grace. They make a difficult, time consuming activity look like a piece of cake while producing extraordinary results. Great leaders know the worth of achieving mastery so they exert time and effort into developing their skills. Many people never reach mastery because they do too many things, most of which are unnecessary. Self-discipline may be applied here by controlling one's emotions and efforts to focus on one thing.

Multi-tasking is great leadership tool but bear in mind that it is only useful when being applied by a specialized skill(skills). This means that when a person wants to achieve more than one goal at the same time, it is more effective to have mastered one way of doing something and apply that way in multiple situations. Imagine a professional musician will have very little result if his To-do List looks like this:

1. Build an ecommerce website that sells musical equipment

2. Write a business plan for a business that sells musical equipment

3. Organize a musical concert

While this looks like an accomplishable list of tasks, a professional musician will find it difficult to accomplish even though he has experience in the three skills required to complete the three goals. Compared to if he employed a web developer in the first task, a professional business writer in the second and an event planner in the third. A good leader will delegate these tasks to the required professionals and focus his effort in areas that requires his specialization. A professional musician will find much ease in accomplishing a list that looks like this:

1. Compile a list of advanced musical equipment necessary that

will be sold on ecommerce site

2. Create a product e.g. music album that will promote the musical equipment to be sold

3. Perform in a musical concert

;As long as there is a sensitive emotion like anger, frustration, desire or anxiety in play, chances are specialization/expertise is not in play. These feelings shouldn't be a motivator to any task because it tampers with mental health and even decision making. These feelings usually come into play when a goal is taking longer to reach than usual. In most cases, a person gives up on a task that is taking too long to achieve, hence, becomes overwhelmed a negative mental state e.g. disappointment and contempt.

Note that this doesn't mean a person shouldn't attempt tasks that requires expertise (which they may not have). Rather, this simply means that a person who doesn't have expertise should expect to spend longer time in achieving a goal than one with expertise. The active word here is 'Expectation'.

A driver with 10 years' experience is by now an expert in driving. Imagine a situation where she is driving and she spots a huge ditch in the middle of the road, requiring her to either maneuver left or right. If she takes left, she may run into an old woman one the sidewalk, and right is a concrete fence. Slowing down is not an option because she is on top speed, neither is running into the ditch. An experienced driver's instinct hold 50% assurance of what option is best executed. The instinct of expert driver on the other hand may be that if she maneuvers left, the old lady on the sidewalk may not be affected, or that maneuvering right will cause very little damage on the car. Either way, her gut feeling/instincts is to be trusted 100%.

Basically, the major difference between experience and expertise in judging whether an instinct is good or bad is the measuring focus on the subject without any implication on distraction. It is necessary for effective results and contributes in managing emotions-consciousness becomes subconscious. 'gut feeling' is stripped off any distractions or interference. A person is better off mastering 2 or 3 skills perfectly and implementing into achieving a specific goal, rather than being a jack of all trades and master of none.

Application of Emotional Maturity- 9 Habits to attaining Emotional Maturity

1. Practice makes perfect. Repeat the same skill over and over again. Remember that while the procedure is recurring, one's emotional consciousness and memory strengthens as well.

2. Set your eyes on the larger picture. Write down a positive affirmation and recite it daily. Consider this exercise as self-hypnosis. This will enable one to appreciate the initial reason for embarking on that task, hence, obedient to one's values. Positive affirmation doesn't only require thinking and speaking good thoughts, it also demands believing. A leader must believe in the course and trust himself to achieving the goal. Affirmations like "I am healthy", "I am successful", "I am great" or even "I will make

the right choices today" will very often manifest with belief.

3. Set boundaries that are healthy. Being emotionally mature means keeping to good habits and restraining from harmful habits. This means to consciously set what and what not to allow. Once this line is defined, defend at all cost. Emotional maturity helps in resisting temptation. It's important to set boundaries because while doing so, one's character and habits are set and likewise emotions are in line. Ensure that other people don't cross your boundaries by being strict with rules. People will obey a person's boundaries if that person is obeying first, else, if you set boundaries and you don't abide by the, no one else will abide.

4. Self-control is an essence that dictate how a person is perceived by others. There isn't any crime in hosting a house party in a quiet neighborhood. But ensure to tune the volume low and wrap everything up before 10pm. Leaders must know when and what. i.e. to explore freedom with caution. In as much as everybody has their human rights, it becomes a crime when it causes harm to somebody else.

5. Learn when to pause and breathe. Rest is vital growth and development process. Our brain serves like a car engine. When it over works itself, it breaks down. It's important to take a break for a few hours in a day (aside the traditional bedtime). This helps to reset one's body and mind.

6. Improve on communication skills. Learn how to listen more and speak less. The ability to discipline self in this way takes emotional maturity. Study people and their environment so that one may become an expert (after much experience in reading people) and maintain excellent relationship.

7. Practice failing forward. Emotional maturity means growing

and developing one's mentality to be resilient. Mistakes are inevitable so don't beat self for not attaining perfection. Encourage self to persist and preserver. By making mistakes, one can easily learn and avoid such mistakes in the future.

8.   Avoid poor decisions. Always consider how a choice will affect your life financial, spiritually and financially. Resist the temptation of instant gratification

9.   Maintain a healthy group. Replace friends if you feel are pulling you back with people who keeps you motivated to attain your goal. There is no need to be sentimental about it except you are willing to sacrifice the life you want for the guilt you think may experience for doing so. In fact, the only thing constant is change.

CHAPTER SIX
ADVANCED MENTAL LEARNING
STRATEGIES

Are there times when your mind shifts from one point to another? Have you had any trouble when focusing on a subject for more than a minute? Are there a bunch of unfinished works littered around your home and a dozen of unrealistic ideas spiral in the wind?

One very powerful tool in a person's life is *the mind*. It takes effort and discipline to master the mind. Imagine going to the gym and you attempt to lift a weight but realize that your arms are too weak so you organize a week routine that helps you strengthen your arms with an overall goal of lifting that weight. That's how the mind works: the mind is also a muscle. And like every other body muscle that requires exercise to function well, the brain also needs its exercise to strengthen Focus and Concentration.

A classic book written by Theron Q. Dumont, shared some basic, helpful brain exercise. It's incredible how these exercises come across as simple and goofy, however, there is a hidden power gotten from practicing them. Imagine the sunrays- compare the heat effect that it produces when focused with a glass towards an object, to the heat when the sun rays are allowed to reflect freely across a surface. The result is a higher degree heat exerted on the focused Sunray. This works the same with giving attention. When attention is fully given to an object, every involuntary and voluntary action will be directed towards achieving interest on the object.

Concentration Exercise

Focused thoughts and action increases chances of acquisition. Although these exercises are monotonous, they produce a greater brain power and capacity. Consider training the body to do the will of the mind in this following exercise (stabilize your mood/feelings to keep neutral):

1.   Sit Still.

Is there a comfortable chair around? Try sitting still on the chair and see how long you can keep still. This exercise may look easy but it isn't. ensure that you aren't making any movement voluntary or involuntary except breathing. Great! If you are able to do this for 5 minutes. In time and with practice, you will be able to sit still for 15 minutes (which is a lot of time to be still without any movement)

2.   fix sight on fingers.

While seated on a chair, keep the head up with chin high and relax your shoulders. Raise the left arm to the level of the shoulder and point to the left direction. While your arm is oscillating from left to right, fix your gaze on the fingers. Let only your head oscillate with your arm while the rest of your body is fixed. Then keep the arm completely still for 1 minute. Over time, you may increase to 5 minute and so forth.

### 3.	Fix gaze on outstretched cup

Fill a cup with water and wrap the cup with your fingers. Raise your grip in front of you and set your gaze on that cup. Maintain a steady posture so not to have any noticeable movements. Practice this exercise for one minute and increase to 5 minutes and so forth. The purpose of this exercise is to win control of involuntary movements. Ensure that all actions are completely involuntary.

### 4.	Open and Close Fist.

Lift your chair onto a table and place your palm on it. Clench your fist while the back of your palm is placed on the table- you thumb over the rest fingers. Now keep your sight on your fist for some time then gradually release your thumb. Ensure to keep all your attention on this action as though it is a matter of extreme importance. Now, gradually release your index finger, then the second, then the third until all fingers are release form tight grip. Reverse this process- closing all fingers in a grip and gradually releasing them one by one. Continue this exercise for at least 5 times. It may be increased to 10 times in a few days. What you will experience at first in practicing this exercise is mind and body fatigue. But by persisting to regulate this exercise in daily life, you can train the brain to persevere in lazy days. Also, it gives control over the muscles and movements. However, it's important that one's gaze is focused on the finger movements in order to rip the full benefits of this exercise.

5.   Increase Sense of Smell.

When passing a meadow of flowers, concentrate on the variety of smells you may detect. What are the different types of order you perceive? It doesn't matter if you don't have the right words to describe them. Select a specific odor out of the variety and focus your senses on that smell. You'll discover that by focusing your attention on that certain smell, the smell become intensified and more predominant than when you didn't put attention on it. When out in the open, ensure to practice this exercise, soon you'll be able to describe more than one specific smell with accuracy.

6.   Inward concentration.

Lay down with you back against your bed, close your eyes and relax the muscle completely. Listen to your heartbeat. Ensure not to pay attention to your surroundings. Think of your inward mechanism; how all your organ is operating greatly by pumping blood to every channel in your body. Try to picture the blood flowing in and out of this great organ to the to the brain, arms, toes etc. focus on the image and listen attentively. With consistent practice, you will actually see and feel the state of your heart.

7.   Focus on Sleep

This is also referred to as the water method as a way of inducing sleep. People find it troubling to intentionally fall asleep. Fill a clear glass with water and place it on a table in your bedroom. Sit on a chair which is placed beside a table and fix your gaze on the glass of water. Think about how calming and serene the water looks. Then imagine yourself falling into the state of the water, feel yourself being calm and serene as well. In time, you will notice your nerves feeling drowsy and sleepy. Cases of insomnia has been resolved because of this exercise. It's a good way to take short naps even when you don't feel like at first.

8.   Talk in front of a glass/mirror

Mark 2 spots on your mirror which is on eye level, consider them as 2 eyes looking back at you. Focus your eyes on the artificial eyes and notice that your eyes blinks at first. Refrain from moving, ensure to stand fixed and erect. Focus your thoughts into the eternal eyes and remain perfectly still. Ensure your head isn't moving. Keep a single thought in your mind and block any other thought. While your mind, emotions and body are fixed at this exercise, still looking at the mirror, imagine yourself to be a reliable and confident person. While on the mirror, inhale a deep breath, hold it in for 3 seconds and release. Ensure that there is enough fresh air in the room. You will discover that your timidity will disappears, it is being replaced by peace and power. Anyone who is able to stand up tall and control facial expressions and moods is always rewarded as the center of attention. Ensure to do this at least 3 minutes a day.

9.   Eastern method of concentration.

Rest uprightly on a chair with a high back. Then press against the left nostril with one finger. Next, inhale very deeply, drawing breath gently as you count to 10. Then release the breath from the left nostril as count another 10. Practice this exercise with the right nostril as well.

10.   Control desire.

Lack of control on desire is a common downfall for many people. It is a difficult force to control. Desires come naturally in many forms. It brews itself from the thoughts and imaginations of a person and only manifests depending on how much energy is concentrated on a certain desire. Positive desires cause positive actions, likewise negative desire cause negative actions. In fact, a positive desire that doesn't have sufficient concentrated energy will produce a negative result.

11.   Reading Exercise.

Nobody can ever concentrate properly on a subject without first acquiring information on that subject. reading helps to fuel the imagination. Every person must train themselves to think clearly and this requires undoubtful data. Always ensure to read at least a page each day. There are a large variety of reading materials, magazines, newspapers, novels, etc., however, don't read carelessly. This means that while reading is important, ensure to read on subjects that are within your niche. Although there is no harm in having a wide span on different subjects, it is always better to concentrate your force at any chance you can get. E.g., a doctor who has an operation the following day, has no business reading an essay about how copper wire is a good insulator.

When you have read, the next step in this exercise is to recite all you've read. Ensure while reading, you are writing. Maybe not word for word but at least, to your understanding. Always remember to keep still during these exercises.

Health is wealth

A person who is aware of his feelings, thoughts and behaviors usually have great emotional health. They know that daily stress and issues are inevitable, so they have devised healthy coping mechanism to deal with them. They are happy and content with self and they maintain good relationships with others.

It is true that many events in life can affect one's emotional wellness. Ineffective management leads to stress, anxiety and depression which are classified as unhealthy state of mind. Note that these feelings are unavoidable and everybody in life is bound to experience them in one way or the order. However, the difference in good and bad emotional health is in how it affects a person's productivity. i.e. you may be having a bad mood but it doesn't necessarily need to affect your work or relationship. Even good/positive can be overwhelming and difficult to manage.

Common experiences that affect emotional states

 I. Getting laid off from work

 II. when your child leaves home/ returns home

 III. when a loved one passes away and one has to deal with it

 IV. getting married or having a divorce

 V. a suffering from illness and injury

 VI. having being promoted at your job

 VII. moving into a new apartment

 VIII. adopting a baby

Your feelings, thoughts and actions affect your body. It is a kind of body-mind connection. In this case, one's behavior begins a subconsciousness that is tied to hat the brain is detecting. Feelings of stress and sadness is a result of a person acting in an absurd way
74

because he feels something is wrong. E.g., stomach ulcer or high blood pressure particularly follows form a shock, such as in a loved one's death.

There are many ways that emotional health can be improved. It's important to first understanding what emotion you feel and why you feel that way. By examining the problem that lead to a certain emotional state, one can easily find a solution that helps keep peace of mind.

How to improve emotional health

Subscribe to appropriate ways to express feelings: if you are experiencing sadness and depression and if it is causing physical damages in your life, it is more harmful when you bottle up these feelings. It's okay to talk about emotions. Talk to somebody that you love and trust but keep in mind that they may not appropriately know the right things to say, so don't be offended when they don't. the goal is not for a solution but an expression of your emotions. By talking about how you really feel, you are able to finally listen to yourself. When you comfortably voice your feelings, you have recognized and admitted the issue which already takes up 50% of the solution.

1. Maintain a balanced lifestyle: refrain from being upset about work, school or domestic issues that leads to negative moods.it doesn't necessarily mean one should fake happiness when feelings of anxiety and stress sets in. it simply means while dealing with these negative emotions, try to focus on the positive feelings, like how will you feel after successfully getting rid of that

troublesome stomach upset? There are many ways to think of all the positive feelings that you feel. Count your blessings. What are you thankful for? It always an advantage to have a journal that you can write all your achievements. It doesn't need to be a huge life changing accomplishment, simple things like visiting the doctor after a long procrastination or learning how to finally ride a bike. They are daily achievements that many of us never stop to notice. If we are thankful for little things, we wouldn't beat ourselves so much, hence, we are in a good mood to accomplish the larger things. Research shows that positive mood has the ability to improve health and extend life.

2. Improve resilience. By acquiring resilience, on is able to cope with overwhelming emotions very easily and healthy. Resilience means elasticity. It is learned and improved by different tactics. It means accepting the unpredictable changes of life, having a positive outlook on yourself, to maintain a healthy support group, having things in a perspective. A counselor or therapist can help in this situation by CBT- "cognitive behavior therapy".

3. Calm the body and mind. Exercise like yoga, meditation, listening to music, tai chi, and listening to imagery sound tracks are very useful when bringing your emotions to balance. Technology has made these materials easily accessible across the globe thanks to the internet. You can find videos on YouTube that helps to relax your moods. By meditating, you are able to guide your thoughts.

4. Pamper yourself. Taking care of yourself is a good sign

of emotional wellness. It's not just the intention that matters but the act of putting in work and attention to living a healthy life. Health is very important to maintain emotional balance. It should reflect in daily routines like exercise, diet plans, rest and relaxation… don't overeat or indulge in drugs and alcohol abuse. There are things to consider when maintaining a healthy emotional state like your body's immune system. A poor state of mind that weaken it. It is what causes a person to get cold/ infections when experiencing emotional difficulties. Have you noticed when feelings of stress, depression and anxiety sets in, you are less likely to take proper care of yourself because you are overwhelmed by emotions, therefore, reasoning is kicked to the wind? You are less enthusiastic about exercising, easting nourishing food (not wallowing in ice-creams and alcohol), or taking your prescribed drugs. It's more likely a person abuse drugs, alcohol and tobacco in this state of emotional insecurity. The other signs that a person is experiencing por emotional health can be seen as thus:

Feelings back discomfort/pain

Alternating appetite (eating too much or too little that usual)

- Chest pain

- Diarrhea/constipation

- Scurvy/dry mouth

- extreme tiredness

- lack of sleep

- headache and dizziness

- sexual complication

- neck stiffens

- stomach upset

- loss of breath

is it necessary to let your doctor know about your emotions?

It's possible that you may not be used to speaking to the doctor about personal life issues. But also remember that he/she can't be aware about your feelings if they aren't told. Emotions aren't quite tangible. It's difficult to mature and quantify feelings like "I feel sad", how sad do you feel? So, don't mind the x-ray if it doesn't pick it up. By being honest with your doctor, you can help prevent complications. First, He/she can ensure your present mental state isn't affecting a physical symptom.

How a person knows when to see a doctor is the point when your negative emotions are strongly expressed by unproductiveness, to the extent you can't seem to enjoy any task, any more. This is what clinical studies call "Major Depression". Depression is a clinical illness that is treated with both medical and individual counseling. You can start with these questions to keep you on track with your doctor:

- How do I cope better when I feel stressed?

- Is my physical health affecting my stress level, or is my stress level affecting my physical health?

- It doesn't feel like I'm stressed, but does my body give symptoms that I am?

- Even though every area in my life is working god, why do I feel unhappy?

Who You Are Is What You Eat.

It's very confusing, and frankly, tiring to keep track on what and what not to eat, especially knowing that 'best diet plan' changes very frequently. However, it's been proven that what we eat affects both how we look physically and how we feel mentally and emotionally. The benefits of improving diet is:

1. Helps in thinking clearly,

2. Keeps you in a good mood

3. Energy booster

An example of how food affects mood is in sugar level. Low sugar level causes tiredness, depression and irritability. By moderately eating carbohydrates which increase sugar level, energy will stabilize. Natural carbohydrates like rice, cereals, bread, nuts, oats, pasta and seeds.

Note: chocolate and ice-cream produce sugar but the energy derived is unsustainable and doesn't contribute to the energy required to complete a task. Also bear in mind that too much intake leads to obesity, which is an unhealthy physical state.

Quick tips for eating healthy:

- Breakfast always sets the day to a great mood. It's what determines the outflow of energy to begin a day.

- Rather than having your meals, lunch and dinner, in large portions, it's better to share them to smaller portions. i.e. 3 large meal to be replaced by 5 small meals in a day

- Keep away from foods that irregulate your body sugar. E.g. chocolates and ice-cream, soda and alcohol.

It's also important to stay hydrated in maintaining good health. Without drinking water regularly, one will find it difficult to think clearly or concentrate on any task. Lack of water causes constipation which is an awful feeling that spoils anybody's mood.

Tips to stay hydrated:

- Drink up to 6-8 glasses of water daily

- Substitute soda for water when thirsty. Water is a cheaper and healthier option.

- Coffee, smoothies, juice and tea are good water intake, however, always be moderate because they contain caffeine or sugar, whereas, water doesn't.

Often times, one's gut reflects on their emotional health. When you are tensed up, it causes your gut to move slowly or fasten up. For proper digestion to occur, ensure to eat fiber foods, drink enough water and exercise regularly. Make gradual changes when changing diet because your gut will take time to adjust to a new plan. Also, if you think that your stress is affecting your gut, then take out time to relax and breathe. It is no wonder that panic attacks are usually corrected with just simply breathing.

Caffeine is considered to be a great energy booster. However, like every other stimulant, it gives an initial high energy boost and when it fades, will leave you feeling anxious and depressed. It causes a person to feel disturbed and experience lack of sleep. A person may experience withdrawal syndrome they suddenly stop taking caffeine. You can find caffeine in tea, chocolate, coffee, cola, and manufactured energy booster drinks. A quick tip for people who are used to drinking tea, cola and coffee is to switch to decaffeinated brands. There is a great noticeable change when a person reduces coffee intake or stops it all together- a person feels better with a lighter mood.

Fruits and vegetables contain lots of vitamins, fiber and minerals that you need to kick the day off to a great start. These are the secret sauce to keeping a steady mental and physical health. By eating a variety of colored fruits, it's impossible not to benefit from a wide range of nourishment. Try to have at least one type of fruit daily, whether tinned, frozen, fresh or a glass of fruit. Ensure to include your vegetables. This is why good planning is necessary. One can benefit from a well-functioning plan where proper attention is given to food menu. Always remember to buy sufficient fruit and vegetables when grocery shopping.

Protein is a major food category. It contains amino acid that formulates the chemicals needed for the functioning of a person's thoughts and emotions. A lot of people don't know that protein meals helps to curb appetite. Proteins can be found in fish, meat, eggs, cheese, soya products, nuts and seeds and in legume (that includes lentils, peas and beans).

Fat and oil are an important class to keep a healthy balanced diet but many people stray away because they fear it will affect their physic. But that's a wrong notion about this glass. There is a good type of fat and bad kinds. Good fats contain fatty acids like omega 3 to help the brain function properly. These healthy fats are contained in foods like poultry meat, oily fish, nuts like walnuts or almonds, olive oils, seeds, avocados, eggs, cheese, yogurt and milk. A good tip to remember is to avoid all 'trans fats' products. There are bad kinds of Fat found in store-bought biscuits and cakes. They can be very tempting, especially when you are experiencing a low mood, however, try to resist or if not, take very little quantity. Let these be a treat that you give yourself once a week.

CHAPTER SEVEN
SELF AND MIND

Many of us go through life with little attention given to our day to day activities. Simple routines like what to have for breakfast or unpredictable events like a construction work that cause road blockage on our journey to work. Our lives are full of events that are connected in a serial order- one event follows another, and we can be present to all, one at a time.

It's better not to think too much about things really. Our wonderful curious mind is better kept to rest rather than to be bothered with ideas that could lead to worries and anxiety. Is it necessary to much the mind above its limit al in the sake of adaptation and acquisition?

But while we debate a proper state of mind, we are as well troubled by our 'self' when we encourage odd thoughts which cross the mind. Self in this context refer to the body and all its organs and mechanism. The mind imposes a powerful effect on self/body. Take caution not to become a victim of mental disturbance, else, the mind becomes one's worst nightmare. In fact, a school of thought considers the mind to be a person's worst enemy regardless of whether the person is mentally fit or not.

Importance of understanding self and mind

It is very useful to distinguish between self (body) and mind. To be in self means to participate in life's complexity and be in the actual world- using the body eye and not the mind's eye. Mind eye is great. The mind is a powerful tool, however, it's the mind that feels and not the body. The mind is vulnerable to circumstances, whereas, the body experience in a more substantial degree. The mind can think all it wants, but if the body doesn't act, nothing is accomplished. Learn to separate both from each other. That's a key to success.

While the body a great medium to action, it is melancholic and not subjective to Dynamic and creativity. Take for example, Linda registered for a gym which she religiously follows routinely. She weighs 150 pounds and her plan is to lose 30 pounds.

This is a practical situation. Since Linda is strict in observing her exercise routine, she will definitely see good result. However, the task will be tedious and feel like a punishment. But what if Linda, while running on the treadmill, begins to imagine herself in a tight bikini suite, on a nice beach while passersby commend her of what a great body she got? The feeling of punishment that traps the body is replaced with hope and aspiration conducted by mind. Here, the mind takes the form of companionship.

But don't be carried away. The mind has a tricky way of tricking one to believe the work isn't necessary. If Linda invest too much attention on the image that her mind creates, and the false feeling of satisfaction that it generates, she may discontinue her routine. This is because she feels satisfied' and this overwhelming feeling may trick the body to believe that it doesn't need exercise to 'be satisfied'.

A most common term used professionally in popular language is "the self". However, the meaning could vary from one context to another. These various meanings about self, are increasingly

84

considered by many as a simple delusional concept that we trick our brain to believe to aid coping with our surroundings. But that's a false accusation. The opposite is an actual truth, that self is an essential and substantial part of all human beings. This argument will be supported by illustrating the complex system and its similarities with the concept of self. This however is not the only way to prove that self is a substantial entity- there are a variety of options, especially from those who subscribe to the concept of mental wellness being reduced by the brain's functionalities. Hence forth, we shall carefully explore two concepts theoretically- first on self and second on the system.

Clinical psychologist finds it increasingly difficult and frustrating because there is no general accepted definition of self as an element behind a medical symptom. Whereas, many symptoms indicated poor cohesiveness of the internal body mechanism. i.e. disordered memories, lack of connection to personal feelings, insecurity and doubt, cognitive unresponsiveness and more. These are obvious links to self as a root sense to a person's being and humanity. Its deficiencies result from loss of management and control leading to a person feeling victimized. It connects to a person's traumatic experiences, por leadership skills or bad emotional state.

It is plausible for psychologist to keep track of the goals to be achieved therapeutically the necessity of restoration and development of the mental structure which are responsible for the mind without too much attention for exclusivity and strict protocols- as in specific oriented therapy. A person should loosely subscribe to therapeutically methods in order to build and develop their mental structure.

Mental structure, or structure in general, here is referred to subjective assumptions and impressions that are applicable to the function of mental works as a whole. This also includes acceptable paradigms that are applicable to therapeutically standards/rules. By the way, popular studies already describe the human being as a psycho-somatic system. So, it's interesting to illustrate the human system in objective perspectives to electrical system- nerves and impulses.

A System in General

The system became an ecological and biological subject of interest in the period of 1943-1953. This leads to cyber studies of basic models and principles of human behavior in society. The basic properties of a system are fundamental to defining the whole in a way they interact individually/characteristically. Unlike treating them separately, their interrelationship is what really matters in terms of definition. The reason the system develops a problem is when it is treated to function separately from the whole. Therefore, a part must be only understood with reference to the whole. Also, there is caution is understanding that one functional part is indeed just another part that have separate function from all other functioning parts.

Not that systems and parts, as used in this context, aren't rigid things. Instead, consider them as an ongoing flow of dynamic interactions among various subsystems in a non-linear network, connecting and formulating structures. Any ongoing activity are referenced to the mechanism of the whole system which is described as a mechanical analytical processing unit.

The autonomy of the system is characterized with boundaries which are within its self-regulating processes. It is structured to foresee a primary purpose of emotional balance and survival. Since it is an opened system, there is a constant inflow of energy that transpires between the system(self/mind) and the surrounding (daily life). This is why the system is better studied and understood while in respect to the surroundings. The power to connect with both people, under a given condition, and to interact specifically is important for all living systems. What generates innovative patterns it's the flexibility of how a person is able to relate. Having a variety of behaviors that doesn't only conform to biological rules and regulations.

The Human System Analogy

Firstly, by applying the general system concept to understand the human system, we must first identify the 'parts. Don't expect it to be an easy process because there are real life controversies about what are the essential human parts.

The whole here is described as the conscious body and the self-conscious body. The body, as playing a part in this system as a whole is still unclear and there are speculations in deducing that the brain is the mind. In which in the analogy of a general system, the mind cannot be the brain. The mind, psyche, self are all mental part of the system and the brain comprise the working part of this system, although this concept is still controversial. Many people will still argue that since mental is connected to physical, the brain is correctly the mind. Others will argue that the through there is a difference, it is not critical but casual and ontological based on the state of being referenced to the whole system, it is only a conscious difference to the person that owns the parts, uses and experience them on a more complex emotional and mental interactions.

Therefore, in this consideration, the mental sense is very different from the biological description as brain- and all biological laws. Since the system here is considered as an open loop that permits the exchange of energy with the surrounding, therefore, the surrounding stimuli is referred to as the third party of the system.

The Mind

As stated in the previous paragraphs, the mind cannot be a tangible entity. It is a process that operates in its highest degree by interaction of system and its environmental stimuli. It reflects the origin of a person and it is subjective to change- change of environment and the development of parts as regards to the whole. It strives in an open system which enables it to ask its own questions, whether irrational or logical unlike a closed system (out of touch of surrounding e.g. brain).While the mind is in touch with its surroundings and perceive the unseen forces like energy, the brain receives these perceptions and ask its own logical questions in trying to analyze data. The mind is the bridge between the brain and the great big world.

The biological description is being aligned parallel with mental descriptions. Clayton-Davies (2006) had formulated this well by stating that the connection between the environment and energy is a mental stimulation and represented by a mental process. In a case like this, its assumed that all mental process produce some criterion in which cognitive structures will play a role that is casual with the environment.it is by virtue that vital mental characteristics which are cognitive processes refers to the pressures, exerted by the surrounding/environment.

Therefore, understand that the self, our consciousness and the mind are all properties that makes up the psycho-somatic system.

It's important to personally take care in observing its interaction amongst each other because it may damage or enhance a person's life. But knowing its origin is always a great way to manage self and mind with the concentration exercise mentioned in the previous chapter. A person is better off with a healthy emotional state when they know how their body operates.

How brain activities process the body senses

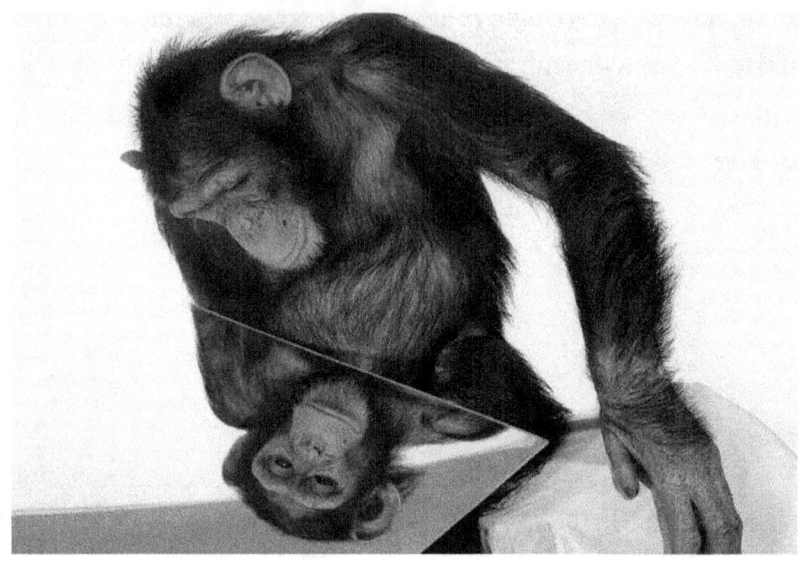

Take a mirror and look into it. You may notice pimples, rashes, wrinkles or uneven facial hair, but right beneath all the imperfections and superficiality is something very interesting. Who is looking back at you in the mirror? The sense of finding self is incredibly divine and unmistakable. It is what makes us human- the very essence of existence that so many fails to notice. However, being aware of self is one of the greatest mind mysteries. What is the origin of self and why is it such a life issue?

When we see other animals' stairs at their reflections, we are reminded that humans aren't alone in the journey of recognizing self. Although, there is a short list of animal species that are able to exercise this recognition ability. Unarguably, it means that the capacity to recognize self, evolved in just the few numbers of high cognitive species with the largest brains. If this is true, mental structural complexity, which is the critical point of consciousness, can be represented in the highest peak.

However, it is discovered that people are beginning to question this idea. A research was carried out that gives ample weight to the nature of self-consciousness and awareness. The experiment involved a monkey specie that earlier scientists deemed as not being able to recognize itself in front of a mirror, but later learnt to do so. This discovery urges all to rethink our understanding about one mind and its self.

The search for self-consciousness amongst other living organism aside humans, has been going on for many decades. One most popular test amongst researchers, on this subject, is the face mark test where researchers apply one spot of a substance, usually a dye that is odorless, on the surface area of an animal's forehead. Then the animal is placed Infront of the mirror and being observed to see its reactions. the result hopes to find that those animals with a strong sense of itself will identify itself in the mirror and try to remove that spot on its face.

Those animals that successfully passed this test is considered to be intelligent species. These animals include bonobos, chimps, elephants (Asian), orangutans, dolphins, killer whales and Eurasian magpies. Here, the correlation of being smart means to be self-aware and generally, has become the criteria for mental complexity. But there is a troubling missing puzzle piece; Gorillas often fail the test with exception to the deceased koko, its noticed that distance relatives(primitive) of this particular specie like the orangutans, always pass the test. Moreover, the so-called self-conscious elites like the pigeons and ants have strange anomalies. Nevertheless, many scientists discredit these smaller organisms of being self-aware. They also explain that the reason why gorillas aren't able to recognize themselves is because they have been mentally depreciating since the separation from their lineage which caused them to have lesser pressure from the environment.

Some years ago, a biological scientist named Liang Tan Change and his colleagues, released a footage from the Shanghai institution. It revealed a small number of rhesus macaques that where interacting with themselves in the mirror. These monkeys where contorting their facial features, stroking their facial hair and tugging the rest of their body parts, and while these behaviors was going on, their eyes were fixed on themselves, in the mirror. It is very clear that they recognize themselves with no doubt. But why has rhesus macaques continually failed this recognition test when previously they had passed. What has changed?

The fact about a Chang's study showed that macaques responded to their images in the mirror after they had been induced with an anecdote and a neural device that was placed on their heads. The group of scientists wondered whether the cause of this specie's lack of self-recognition was due to lack of coordination of the mind. Lack of coordination of mind in this context refers to when the body movement doesn't correlate with what is being seen and perceived. This was tested by training the monkey's to properly express themselves by touching a laser dot- if done well, the monkeys are given food treats. At first it was completely impossible, the monkey's d=refused the laser dot because they couldn't see it. Then the researchers increased the intensity so be well visible to the monkeys. Few weeks later, after vigorous practices, these species successfully passed their recognition text with incredible results.

This is a wakeup call that the way self-conscious/awareness test is flawed. Hence, self-awareness is a complex subject that shouldn't be approach in a linear manner.

Stages of Consciousness

Many psychologists are convinced that the brain's consciousness and complexities correspond differently from on individual to another, respective to hierarchy placement. The minimum level at its base it assigned to animals with a simpler nervous system. A simpler nervous system is assumed to be more distance with his nerves and hence less sensitive to daily encounters. Animals with low level of consciousness find it difficult to use their senses in identifying colors, when they experience hunger; when they feel cold; or when they become scared. Their brain simply processes these senses with less concern. The leader's mind is sophisticated and sensitive enough to experience the world in a more conscious manner through a more perspective lens. Although their senses are still limited to a distinctive sense of self. Its only at the highest point of self-consciousness that we can discover our mind's ability to structure a lifetime of self-centered concepts. These minds are referred to as 'the elites'

How is this hierarchy made and what is its criteria? Because the subject of the mind' complexity is so vague and nobody can truly see and understand the workings of another person's mind, talk less of the minds of other animals like ants and bats. This difference arise from the various evolution needs which most animals must reach to survive. E.g. oysters just have two clustered cells that makes up its nervous system. This enables it to perform exactly how an oyster ought to perform-managing digestion and signal transmission from its tentacles to its muscles which reacts by snapping itself shut when a predator is in a critical close range. But there seem to be a particular demanding behavior that led to the evolution of the complex brain, which is responsible for creating self. It is in the act of dealing with other people's mind; in becoming the prey, or the competitors or a member of the social group.

Robin Dunbar had created a social interactive brain hypothesis at Oxford University- life in a tightly woven community, particularly produce greater challenges due to the expectations of close relationships which clings to the idea of an importance in understanding the mechanism of another person's mind. In other for a person in society to acquire this necessary skill, the brain must evolve to the complexity so as to be sensational and observant to his surroundings. According to Michael Grazino, a neuroscientist at Princeton University, high consciousness requires building a mind model. The evolution of this mind model by biological mechanics, helps to easily understand both the mind of self and that of others.

Whatever the need may be, whether for mind reading or television broadcasting, models are usually based on factors that surround is points of interests and relevance to the system in question. A simulation being ran, depends on the quantity of the result as it relates to the specified requirements (observative, modification and assumption)- permitting a reasonable prediction and conclusion. This is usually accurate and thus represents a more reliable model to apply in subjective experiments. Gaziano says that the braid is a model-builder. It's impossible to move a finger if the motor cannot locate where it is, or predict where it is going in a few seconds it cannot run or comprehend how it will send a signal to the brain in other for it to function properly. Gaziano also argues that the level of social interaction and understanding people is also applicable to how the brain uses this mechanism to survive. It's possible that self-awareness is just a hall of mirrors and not a simulation.

It is safe to say that in human beings, self-awareness is the state of a person's mind that is conscious and sensational, being able to simulate with another person's mind. There is no need to extrudate its importance. Self-consciousness doesn't necessarily mean higher-order, or intelligence, or complexity that self-awareness. They are one and the same. The mind itself is another form or entity that the brain is able to model and manipulate to its use. It is difficult to speculate if these activities work with respect to unique biological complexities. Afterall, it is still a mystery to what consciousness looks like in our own and other people's brains.

Many researchers will conclude that our brain works partly by generating stimulus, but then, disagree about the consciousness being a functional part of the brain model. Instead, it is seen as an unintentional rush of emotions through a closed loop of brainly connections. Consciousness is unable to not exist even not serving any specific purpose. Its analogy is linked to the noise from a car engine- there is no particular reason for the noise, without the noise, it will still function well, although the noise is a great sign that the car engine is turned on.

We can see many examples of this concept in nature which gives an impression of the brain's complexities, even though the whole system doesn't know how to operate intentionally, and with respect to the concept itself. An example can be seen in a flock of birds and their interactive behaviors, using a model that has an individual drive only two opposing forces. They possess an instinct that urges them to follow their neighbor birds and to back off when they get so close. These complexities can also be recognized in Petri-dish-bound colonies, where bacteria respond automatically to a chemical stimulus which is secreted by other bacteria in the colony, for proximity regulation. This model in the case of the birds and bacteria, has no specific purpose. It is just an indicator to show how each individual poses a certain force.

No doubt that self-awareness is a complex phenomenon that originates from the brain. But a mind is unable to identify or observe its personal components. It is only able to form a model by the adaptation of millions of electric stimuli which the environment generates. The signal flows in a more dynamic way, and rushing through connected moments with the surrounding. However, some parts of the brain in different animal, flows better than others. Humans experience this differentiation in predominant links that seem to be more familiar with reasoning other people's minds, and reasoning with the same methods, our own minds. The result forms the model.

CONCLUSION

Many people are victims of settling for an unhappy life not because they want to but rather, a sense of helplessness about their circumstances. They don't think it's possible to change moods so easily, they think it's a difficult and even worse, an impossible task. Guess what! It's not even a task at all, it's just a way of life. The way an unhappy mind works is that it thinks its circumstances are divine- that their mental suffering is punishment from the Gods for being naughty at one point in their lives. An unhappy mind always focuses on the negative. The problem is that they are looking for happiness in the wrong places.

Don't be surprised that even the rich cry. Happiness is not materialistic/tangible, so therefore, it cannot be bought. And is it not bizarre that while some rich people experience extreme sadness in their lives, some of the lowest income earning people go by their lives feeling very fulfilled and satisfied? Forget about 'stuff' and acquisition, happiness comes from within.

By making conscious decision that leads to happiness, one will definitely realize it. By constantly seeking for something, it's inevitable to discover it. That's just how the system we call the great big world works. Don't be deceived that happiness is a natural phenomenon, just like everything other goals we aspire in our lives, happiness also requires effort. But no worries, it's not a mounting moving type of energy you need, just a little bit of your energy that matter. Put in that little effort to becoming a better person everyday- who doesn't want to be a better version of themselves? The fact is that your better version is 100% useful both to yourself and others.

This has nothing to do with perfection, it's more to do with caring for your health- mentally, physically and emotionally. Although a happy state doesn't mean complete eradication of unhappy feelings. Having predominant unhappy emotions causes harm to both a person and the environment. Unhappy people are always to be avoided- nobody likes to be around negative energy. Leaders ensure to be on their brightest mood- not faking but genuine happy feelings. They are able to discipline their selves by these simple daily acts in which the reward promises a serene, peaceful and happy life.

HOW TO ENJOY A HAPPIER LIFE IN 60 WAYS

1. Genuinely listen to people. Don't just 'hear' them, waiting for when they finish so you can begin speaking? There is so much to learn from others. Many people just want to be listened to, they don't really care about your advice or opinion, they just want to feel heard and being that support system adds value to the relationship. Wouldn't you like to be a cause of value?

2. Venture into something nice not for yourself now, but for someone else. This is similar to the first act but in this case, you are doing something tangible that the person can acknowledge and appreciate. Run an errand for a friend, buy a gift for a loved one, and cover a shift. The simple things are what really counts.

3. Have a list of all the things you are grateful for. You can write and rewrite the list every week, putting into more

items.

4. Try to stretch and take in long breaths. do this at least 2 minutes daily

5. Ensure to meditate daily. The best time to meditate is first thing in the morning and last thing before bed. It's a comforting mind exercise that always helps one feels good about a sense of direction.

6. Escape from egocentrism. Ones ego is a trap. It's the death of self which prevents one from having a healthy social relationship with others.

7. Ensure to read a great book daily. Books are powerful media for knowledge. Even if it's a paragraph or a page- a whole chapter? That's great. But don't make it into a serious task, else, it loses the magic.

8. Don't consume negative information. Whether from books, the internet or from someone else. Negative news are mood spoilers.

9. Create quality time for family. Do this each day. If they are far away, call or text them and let them know that you care

10. Take long walks

11. Have a meet up with close friends at least once a week.

12. Ensure to floss. If you can't religiously do a simple task like flossing, then other areas of your life may need to be rechecked in terms of dedication.

13. Nobody likes a gossip. Never gossip.

14. Acceptance is the first step to change. It's okay to aspire for more but it's wise to appreciate what you have. It doesn't

mean settling but rather, contentment.

15. Keep a to-do list, in the form of a journal and update daily

16. Put in passion in all that you do. Whatever it be that exhaust your time daily, ensure to make it worth the while.

17. Subscribe to the news. When you are well informed about your surroundings, you have better chances in navigating through successfully.

18. Avoid processed food. Learn how to eat a good meal.

19. Charity rewards with a feeling of fulfilment.

20. Planning is always better than not because one is able to manage their time efficiently.

21. Always keep positive people around and avoid the negative people.

22. Start your day early. It's incredible how much you can get done by waking an hour or 2 hours earlier.

23. Don't over work yourself

24. Don't brag about your accomplishment. Nobody wants to hear all of that. Let your accomplishments show for itself. If you put in so much work as you claim, your efforts will speak for itself- people will read through you.

25. Learn to laugh. Not little, laugh a lot.

26. Volunteer for a course.

27. Stop giving too much thought about other's thoughts of you. Everybody has an opinion, so you can't please everybody- that's too stressful in trying to do so. To keep happiness, you must appreciate individualism in respect to self and mind.

28. Stop worries. Many awful things that we think about are never going to really happen, so why stress on the matter? Worries is never the answer to a problem. By worrying about an issue, you go through the effect twice.

29. It's never too late. The only real deadline is death.

30. Age is just a number, stop obsessing about getting old.

31. Play a little. Life is not that serious

32. The mind is a tricky place to venture alone. Talk to someone you trust about what's bothering you. It could be a friend or a professional, whoever it is, make that move when you have the slightest feeling that the problem is too large to endure.

33. Fear is a natural phenomenon- it causes a fight or flight reaction, however, don't let the feeling consume your mind to the extent of paralysis. What doesn't kill you only makes you stronger.

34. Avoid setting unrealistic expectations from yourself and others. By expecting too much from others, it stirs resentments.

35. Admit ignorance. It's very admirable when a person is able to say that they don't know something too well or at all. It shows confidence of self. Moreover, by admitting not to understand something, it creates an opportunity to learn.

36. Have kids- they bring joy. If you think kids are too much work, then keep a pet care for it

37. Don't use unnecessary buzz-words.

38. Don't be a stranger to others. Give thoughtful compliments

39. Keep the door held for the person walking behind you.

Courtesy demands it.

40. Say please and thank you

41. Stay positive. Sometimes, terrible things occur, which is normal to grieve, take your time and grieve and when that is done, bounce back to your positivity.

42. Be dedicated with your task. Submit yourself fully to the present.

43. Have a consistent character. Although it's nice to be spontaneous, but don't let it to the extreme where people around you begins to questions your Genuity.

44. Avoid stepping on people's toes, apologize when you do.

45. Be punctual. Don't be late for anything. It's not 'cool', rather its perceived as disrespectful

46. Live up to your words. Practice what you preach and let others admire you for that.

47. You don't need to put another person down just to feel good about yourself

48. Live in the present and connect with the real world. Reduce your presence on virtual world like social media and the internet. Rather than face time, meet up with buddies, especially when they are only a few miles away.

49. Advice that are unsolicited are never really appreciated. Avoid dishing them if the real purpose is just to make you feel good about yourself and not to really help the other.

50. Rather that showing pity, have empathy. People are prone to be defensive on acts of pity. It's a way of indirectly accusing them of weakness. Everybody likes to show strength and

courage in difficult times so let them be. Rather than give thoughtless condolence, for example, when a person loses a loved one. Don't just say "sorry for your loss", let them know that you actually feel their grieve by adding "sorry, you pain gives me much sadness" or instead, "it's a pity that the world has lost someone so precious".

51. Avoid spoiling and pampering kids. It wouldn't help them at all. Instead, exercise proper discipline and give rewards and punishment here necessary.

52. When missed a call, text or return back. Don't you hate when you call somebody, they don't pick up, and neither do they return the call? Especially when you need to pass an important message. It's a different situation when you intentionally don't want to pick up(which is still an unhealthy way to deal with a breakup)

53. Don't over eat. There is an awful feeling of being overweight. Suddenly clothes don't fit, the stairs now become Mount Everest, instant gratification with a sour after feeling. It's better to substitute junks with healthy snack that curbs appetite. Also drinking Tea helps to keep the mouth busy.

54. Avoid procrastination. Procrastination is the death of soul. Nothing important is ever done, which leaves a person feeling unaccomplished.

55. Stay humble. Everybody who are on the top of their game exercise humility very well. Notice how great people appear very simple. They aren't extravagant with their choice of clothes, neither will you see them bragging on social media about their accomplishments.

56. Have a mental picture of your life purpose. Even though it may be unclear at first, meditation will make it clearer. Having a purpose gives us something to look forward to when we wake in the morning.

57. Be honest with your feelings. If someone offends you, don't be afraid to express how you really feel, but take caution with your manner. Two wrongs don't make a right. Even if you lie about how you feel, others can instantly sense it and may tag you as a dishonest person.

58. It's okay to make mistakes. Avoid being too hard on others. Most especially, don't be hard on yourself. No one is above mistakes and the sooner you realize that, the simpler it becomes to handling disappointments.

59. Treat everybody equally. This is a truce reflection on your character. Don't disrespect the janitor and praise the CEO. Learn to understand that everybody is a part of a system and are necessary to have the system work effectively. Therefore, don't discriminate but rather appreciate.

60. Forgive and let go of painful memories. It's not as simple as it sounds but it's achievable by learning to practice the previous behaviors so that over time, the wound will heal.